Infant Communion

Post-Reformation to Present-Day

by

Mark Dalby

Archdeacon Emeritus of Rochdale

Contents

THE COVER PICTURE
portrays Frank (in his mother's arms) and Sebastian Morée receiving
communion at their baptism at Pentecost 2008, St. Mary Magdalene,
Prague, and is reproduced by permission of the boys' parents and the
photographer, Petr Peták. It is supplied by David Holeton (just visible with
back to camera), the Anglican theologian who has been a pioneer in the
restoration of infant communion.

First Impression May 2009

ISSN 0951-2667

ISBN 978-1-85311-998-9

Introduction

In *Infant Communion: The New Testament to the Reformation* I expressed the hope that I could extend the Study to our own times.[1] This essay fulfils that hope. But, while from at least the third to the thirteenth centuries infant communion was widely practised, in the period of the present Study its practice was largely confined to the east. With a few notable exceptions, the west accepted the medieval and reformation consensus that it was at best inappropriate or at worst impossible. I have recorded such references and debates as I have found, but their tone was often desultory. Most recently, however, the old consensus has been vigorously challenged and, if the previous Study began with the practice of infant communion and ended with its abandonment, the present Study begins with that abandonment as a 'given' but concludes with the beginnings of a revival.

Mark Dalby

December 2008

---

[1] Mark Dalby, *Infant Communion: The New Testament to the Reformation* (Alcuin/GROW Joint Liturgical Study 56, Grove Books, Cambridge, 2003) p.2.

1. The First Hundred Years

Although the west had abandoned infant communion there was still awareness of the eastern practice[2], and in 1582 Jeremiah II of Constantinople, presented with a translation of the Augsburg Confession, emphasized its importance on the basis of John 6.53.[3]   Fifty years later Metrophanes Critopoulos of Alexandria urged that infants should communicate as often as their parents wished.   If the western objector was anabaptist, 'we use against him the texts "Suffer the little children to come unto me and forbid them not" and "Except ye eat the flesh of the of the Son of Man and drink his blood ye have no life in you"'   If he was not anabaptist 'we use against him the arguments which he uses against them.'[4]   The reformed writer Herman Witsius sought to answer Metrophanes[5], but the west in general avoided his challenge.   Jacques Goar, a French liturgist, noted only that for 'fear of accidents' the Latins think that infants cannot be admitted 'without scandal'[6], while Abraham Ecchellensis[7], a Maronite, and Leo Allatius[8], a Greek catholic, cited the east's alleged communicating infants in one kind as proof of its basic doctrinal similarity with Rome.

The Lutheran Martin Chemnitz irenically declared that on infant communion 'there is no controversy between us and the Romans'[9], but Theodore Beza, Calvin's successor at Geneva, complained that the Lutheran concept of infant faith led logically to infant communion.[10] Zachary Ursinus in a commentary on his 1562 Heidelberg Catechism

[2]   Cf Jerome Osorius, *De Rebus Emmanuelis* (Lisbon, 1571) p.353; Edward Brerewood, *Enquiries touching the Diversity of Languages and Religions*, xxii, xxiv, xxv (London, 1622) pp.157, 172, 178; Peter Heylyn, *Cosmography*, fifth edn (London, 1682) bk.3 pp.40, 121, bk 4 pp.6, 50, and *Mikrokosmos*, eighth edn (Oxford, 1639) p.344.

[3]   Jeremiah II, *Censura Orientalis Ecclesiae ad Germanos* (Dillingen,1582) ch.9, p.127.

[4]   Metrophanes, 'Confessio Catholicae et Apostolicae in Oriente Ecclesiae' in H. Weissenborn and E.J. Kimmel (eds), *Monumenta Fidei Ecclesiae Orientalis* (Jena, 1850) ii.125.

[5]   Herman Witsius, *The Economy of the Covenants between God and Man*, Vol.II, ET (London, 1837) pp.455f, cited by R. S. Rayburn, 'Report of the Ad-Interim Committee to study the Question of Paedocommunion: Minority Report' (1988) in *Position Papers* (PCA Historical Centre, St Louis, Missouri, 2003) pp.504ff.

[6]   Jacques Goar, *Euchologion*, second edn (Venice, 1730) p.306.

[7]   Abraham Ecchellensis, *Notae ad Arabicos canones concilii Nicaeni* xvii, in P. Labbe and G. Cossart (eds), *Sacrosancta Concilia* (Paris, 1671-73) ii.409.

[8]   Leo Allatius, *De Ecclesiae Occidentalis atque Orientalis Perpetua Consensione* bk.3 ch.15 n.6 (Cologne, 1648) col 1192.

[9]   Martin Chemnitz, *Examen Concilii Tridentini* (1565-73) (Berlin,1861) p.381.

[10]   Theodore Beza, *Responsio ad Acta Colloquii Montisbelgardensis* (Geneva, 1588) p.100.

disagreed.   Baptism was 'an entrance and receiving, or a sign of receiving into the Church', but the supper was 'a sign, whereby God might confirm and seal unto us, that he having once received us into the Church, will also evermore preserve us in it ... and also that he will continue his benefits once bestowed upon us, and will cherish and nourish us by the body and blood of Christ'.   He added, 'This they who are of age and understanding stand in need of, to be a confirmation unto them, as who are diversely tempted.   As for Beza,

> 'Unto baptism regeneration sufficeth by the holy Ghost, or an inclination to faith and repentance.   In the Supper are added and required conditions, which hinder the use thereof to be granted unto Infants ...
> (1) That they who use the sign, shew forth the death of the Lord.
> (2) That they try themselves, whether they have faith and repentance or no.'[11]

The supper required not just an infant's 'inclination' to faith, or faith 'in possibility' but rather an 'actual faith, which is a knowledge, confidence, beginning of obedience, and a serious and earnest purpose to live well', and this infants did not have.[12]

The Lutheran J.A. Quenstedt also took up Beza's challenge and complained that he had used against infant communion the arguments which anabaptists used against their baptism.   Like Ursinus he stressed that the eucharist was 'a sacrament not of investiture and initiation but of confirmation', and he also claimed that Matthew 28.19 constituted a command to admit infants to baptism, whereas there was no such command to admit them to the supper.[13]

In 1595 Rudolph Hospinian in Zurich summed up the protestant objections:
> Neither the custom nor its necessity has any firm foundation in the word of God.
> Children cannot prepare by self-examination and, if they were admitted without this, adults might be less careful about their own self-examination.
> One who dies without the eucharist 'is not deprived of the true sharing of the body and blood of Christ if he has been made a member of Christ by baptism.'

---

[11]   Zachary Ursinus, *The Sum of Christian Religion* (ET by H.Parry, Oxford, 1591) pp.673f.
[12]   *ibid.* p.710.
[13]   J.A.Quenstedt, *In Systemate Theologica* (Wittemberg, 1641) pp.376f.

The supper is of value only to those who can understand it and who can personally fulfil its requirements by remembering the Lord's death and examining themselves.

The passover and the supper are related as circumcision and baptism, but the passover was open only those able to ask, 'What mean ye by this service?'

John 6 refers to spiritual rather than sacramental eating.

The covenant which enabled infants to be baptized did not offer them access to the supper. The purpose of the supper was different and 'all those things which are expressly required for the supper are not so strictly required for baptism.' To defer till its proper time what in infancy was neither convenient nor profitable involved them in no loss.[14]

The French protestant, Philippe Duplessis-Mornay, dismissed the infant communion attested by Augustine as 'but the doting devotions of some particular persons.'[15] Another Frenchman, Jean Daille, used it to support his argument that the Fathers had erred, with both Romans and protestants 'rejecting such of their opinions and practices as are not suited to their taste.' On Trent's denial that they had taught the necessity of infant communion he claimed that either Trent 'has made that which has been, to be as if it had never been' or, more probably, that 'the Fathers of this council, either out of forgetfulness or otherwise, mistook themselves.'[16]

For the Romans, John Maldonatus admitted that for six hundred years the eucharist had been held 'necessary even for infants', but he agreed with Trent that it was not necessary and should not be given to them.[17] Robert Bellarmine denied that Augustine deemed it necessary for salvation: 'The eucharist was instituted to preserve and nourish the spiritual life acquired in baptism, as physical food, which preserves natural life, acts in the physical sphere.'[18] Hence

'As one can live for some time without food, at least until the natural heat begins to destroy the vital liquid, so the spiritual life can be preserved without the eucharist until the heat of

---

[14]   R.Hospinian, *Historia Sacramentaria* (Zurich, 1595) bk 2, pp.59-61.
[15]   P.Duplessis-Mornay, *De L'Eucharistie* (1598) - ET *Of The Institution, Use and Doctrine of the Holy Sacrament of the Eucharist* (London, 1600) bk 1 c.6, p.52.
[16]   J.Daille, *Traite de l'employ des saints peres*, 1632, bk.1 ch.8, bk.2 ch.4, bk.2 ch.6, ET T. Smith rev G. Jekyll (London, 1843) pp.64, 130, 275, 307.
[17]   J.Maldonatus, *Commentarii in Quatuor Evangelistas* (1595f) on Jn 6.53, paras 111, 113 and 116 (Paris, 1629) cols.1486-88.
[18]   R.Bellarmine, *Disputationes de Controversiis* (1586-93) bk 4 c.7 (ed Cologne, 1628) iii.491.

concupiscence begins to devour the waters of grace and virtue. But this happens not in infancy but in adulthood, and to show that the eucharist was not instituted for infants the Lord himself instituted it not in milk, which is the food of infants, but in bread and wine which are rightly only for adults.'[19]

Jacques Duperron, replying to Duplessis-Mornay, commented that 'Augustine would not have thought that to eat the flesh of Christ and to drink his blood was no more than to recall in thought and memory the story of his death, for little children lack knowledge and would be incapable of these.' He saw no need to discuss whether the church then regarded infant communion as necessary since 'our opponents do not attribute this sense to it'.[20] But Ludovic Cellotius admitted that Augustine and others had seemed to make the eucharist as necessary as baptism, though the universal church had never received this doctrine.[21]

In England the Puritan Thomas Cartwright described infant communion as 'a horrible abuse' resulting from Augustine's misinterpretation of John 6.53[22], and William Fulke accused Augustine and Innocent of teaching that infants who had not received the supper 'were damned'.[23] There were further slighting references[24], and Richard Field bluntly dismissed the eastern practice as 'an error'.[25]

Sadly, Richard Hooker made no reference to infant communion, but he argued that while 'the same effects and benefits which grow unto men by the one sacrament may rightly be attributed unto the other', yet each had that 'which is peculiar unto itself'. Thus 'we receive Christ Jesus in baptism once as the first beginner, in the eucharist often as being by

[19]   *ibid.* bk 1 c.9, *ed.cit.* iii.69.
[20]   J.Duperron, *Réfutation de toutes les objections tirées des passages de sainct Augustin alléguez par les hérétiques contra le sainct sacrament de l'eucharistie* in *Les Diverses Oeuvres* (Paris, 1622) pp.100f.
[21]   L.Cellotius, *Notae ad Walterii Aurelianensis Episcopi Capituala*, PL 119.734f.
[22]   T.Cartwright, *Reply to the Answer* in J.Ayre (ed), *J. Whitgift:Works* (Cambridge, 1851-53) ii.521f.
[23]   W.Fulke, 'Discovery of the Dangerous Rock of the Popish Church' in R Gibbings (ed), *Answers* (Cambridge, 1848) p.392.
[24]   Cf Andrew Willet, *Synopsis Papismi* (London, 1592) p.429; anon, 'Answer to Cooper' in J. Strype, *Annals of the Reformation* (Oxford, 1824) ll.i.293; David R. Holeton, 'Communion of All the Baptized and Anglican Tradition' in *Anglican Theological Review* LXIX (1987), reprinted in Ruth A. Meyers (ed), *Children at the Table* (Church Publishing, New York, 1995), adds (p.20) Thomas Morton, *A Catholicke Appeal for Protestants* (London,1610) pp.136-38, 244f and *Of the Institution of the Sacrament of the Blessed Bodie and Blood of Christ* (London, 1631) pp.38-40, and William Ames, *A Fresh Suit against Human Ceremonies in Gods Worship* (London, 1633) pt.2, p.37.
[25]   R.Field, *Of the Church* iii.9 (Cambridge, 1847-52) i.177f.

continual degrees the finisher of our life.'[26] William Barlow wrote of Christ being present in both: 'in them both we communicate with him; bred anew in the one, fed anew in the other.'[27] Some saw the supper as a renewal or confirmation of the baptismal covenant.[28] But William Pemble stated that God 'hath in the manner of their institution, made a plain difference of the persons that are to partake of them.'[29] Thomas Bedford asserted that 'Baptism is for Admission and Regeneration; the Lord's Supper for Confirmation and Preservation'[30], and Ussher declared that the supper was 'to strengthen and continue' the life received in baptism: 'In Baptism our Stock of life is given us, by the Sacrament it is confirmed and continued.'[31]

William Bedell was more ambiguous. He saw the sacraments 'as seals, to confirm the Covenant, not to confer the promise immediately', and he thought that Augustine's anti-Pelagian writings on infant baptism could be disregarded since he 'says the like of the Eucharist also touching the necessity and efficacy in the case of infants.'[32] When challenged as to the necessity of infant baptism if it produced no effect till years of discretion, he replied,

> 'Though the most principal effect be not attained presently, the less principal are not to be refused. So children were circumcised, which could not understand the reason of it, and the same also did eat the Passover. And so did also children baptized in the primitive Church communicate in the Lord's Supper, which I know not why it should not be so still.'

If, as his correspondent suggested, baptism took away original sin and this principal effect was attained immediately,

> 'By this doctrine, you must also maintain, that children do spiritually eat the flesh of Christ and drink his blood, if they receive the Eucharist, as for divers ages they did, and by the analogy of the

---

[26] R. Hooker, *Laws of Ecclesiastical Polity* V.lvii.6, in J. Keble (ed), *Works*, (Oxford, 1850) ii.4; cf also V.lxvii.1, ii 80.

[27] W.Barlow, *A Defence of the Articles of the Protestant Religion* (London, 1601) pp.124-27.

[28] William Perkins, *The Foundation of Christian Religion* in I.Breward (ed) *Works* (Sutton Courtenay Press, Appleford,1970) p.164; James Ussher, *A Body of Divinity* (London, 1645) p.422; Robert Harris, *Treatise of the New Covenant* (1634) in *Works* (London, 1635) p.583; Thomas Bedford, *A Treatise of the Sacraments* (London, 1639) p.103.

[29] W.Pemble, *Vindiciae Gratiae* (London, 1627) pp.49f.

[30] T.Bedford, *op.cit* p.204-06.

[31] James Ussher, *Sermon XIII* in *Eighteen Sermons* (London, 1660) p.448.

[32] W.Bedell, 'Letters' in E.S. Shuckburgh (ed), *Two Biographies of William Bedell* (Cambridge, 1902) *Ep.xxxvii* (2 Apr 1630) to Ward, p.301.

Passover they may (perhaps ought) since they do not *ponere obicem contrariae cogitationis et pravae operationis.* And since the use of this sacrament *toties quoties* must needs confer grace, it seems it were necessary to let them communicate (and the oftener the better to the intent they might be stronger in grace) which opinion, though St Augustine and many more of the Ancients maintain, I believe you will not easily condescend unto.'[33]

Joseph Hall also criticized Augustine: he who held it impossible for an unbaptized child to be saved 'held it also as impossible, for the same infant, unless the sacramental bread were received into his mouth.' There was 'the same ground for both, the same error in both', and since 'both cannot stand, both will fall together for company.'[34] But while Hall upheld infant baptism he described it as 'a weak misprision, to cram the Blessed Eucharist into the mouths of infants.'[35]

Some writers were still concerned primarily to embarrass the Romans.[36] But John Cosin acknowledged that infant communion had been abolished 'by the consent of the whole Western Church' and that here 'we are beholden to the Church of Rome'.[37] He later noted, however, that even for infants the ancient church administered baptism immediately before the supper: they were 'the twin-sacraments, and therefore go together'.[38] But the Puritans were now less concerned to embarrass Rome than to refute the baptist charge of inconsistency, and this controversy and its wider implications have been carefully studied by David R. Holeton.[39] Daniel Featley repeated that 'baptism is a sacrament of initiation, the Lord's Supper of perfection.'[40] Stephen Marshall noted that scripture was

---

[33] W.Bedell, *Ep xliii* (14 Nov 1630) to Ward, *ibid* pp.319-23.

[34] J.Hall, *Epistles, Fifth Decade* iv (1611) in P.Hall (ed), *Works* (Oxford, 1837) vi.248f. On Augustine, cf also J. Prideaux, *Fasciculus Controversarium Theologicarum* (Oxford, 1649) p.286.

[35] J.Hall, *Cheirothesia* (1649), *ibid*, x.454.

[36] cf William Chillingworth, *An Answer to some passages in Rushworth's Dialogues* in *Additional Discourses* (London, 1719) p.53, and Lord Falkland, *Discourse on Infallibility, with an Answer to it and his Lordship's Reply*, (London, 1651) *Reply* p.82.

[37] J.Cosin, *Notes and Collections on the Book of Common Prayer'*, First Series, *Works* (Oxford, 1855) v.144-46.

[38] *ibid*, Third' Series, *Works* v.482.

[39] D.R.Holeton, *art.cit.* p.21-28 where he quotes the Baptist writers Edward Barber, *A Small Treatise of Baptisme, or Dipping* (London, 1641) p.18; Henry Haggar, *The Foundation of the Font Discovered* (London, 1653) pp.66f, and John Tombes, *Anti-paedobaptisme* (London, 1654) p.37; cf also his *Infant Communion - Then and Now*, (Grove Liturgical Study 27, Grove Books, Bramcote, 1981) pp.16-20.

[40] D.Featley, *The Dippers Dipt* (London, 1645) pp.62f.

'altogether silent' about infant communion[41], though John Geree dismissed it as 'inconsistent with the Word'.[42]   But occasionally there were hints of a more nuanced position.   Thomas Blake contrasted the passivity of the baptizand with the activity of the communicant[43], John Brinsley declared that 'infants have a right to it, but not in it'[44], and Richard Baxter explained that it was 'for want of natural capacity to use the ordinance, and not for want of a right if they had such capacity' that infants were not admitted.[45]

Meanwhile the controversy had spread to New England where Thomas Shepard argued strongly for children's church membership.   But not all members enjoyed the same privileges, 'for a man may speak and prophesy in the Church, not women'.   Children enjoyed some privileges, 'even that of baptism'.   But the supper 'doth not seal up this first entrance and first right to the covenant, but our growth and fruition of the covenant', hence the need for self-examination 'and the act of taking and eating Christ, and of discerning the Lord's body, and doing this in remembrance of Christ.' Thus

> 'A child may receive a promise aforehand of a rich estate given him, and this promise sealed up to him, his father receiving it for him; but it is not fit that he should be put to the actual improvement and fruition of that estate until he is grown up, understands himself, and knows how to do it: so it is here; the sacrament of the Lord's Supper requires ability, (1) To take Christ as our own;   (2) To eat Christ; that is, to take fruition of Him; the which acts of faith God doth not require of all those immediately who are wrapped up in covenant with Him.'[46]

[41]   S.Marshall, *A Sermon of the Baptizing of Infants* (London, 1644) pp.51f.
[42]   J.Geree, *Vindiciae Paedo-Baptismi* (London, 1646) pp.53f.
[43]   T.Blake, *The Birth Privilege* (London, 1644) pp.18f.
[44]   J.Brinsley, *The Doctrine and Practice of Paedo-Baptism Asserted and Vindicated* (London, 1645) pp.34-36, 61-64.
[45]   R.Baxter, *Certain Disputations of the Right to the Sacraments* iii (London, 1657) p.294.
[46]   T.Shepard, 'The Church Membership of Children' in I. H. Murray (ed) *The Reformation of the Church* (Banner of Truth, London, 1965) pp.383-405, esp pp.395-97.

2. Deeper Discussion

Deeper discussion began in 1647 when Jeremy Taylor rejected Augustine's description of infant communion as 'an apostolic tradition'[47] and sought to refute the anabaptist charge.[48]   He later explained that its early practice and subsequent abandonment was an illustration of the rightful authority of the church where there was no commandment of Christ.   There was 'infinitely more reason, why infants may be communicated, than why they may not be baptized'[49] and in the primitive church 'nothing was of absolute necessity but innocence and purity from sin, and a being in the state of grace'[50].

In 1660 Taylor offered his fullest discussion.   The primitive church had deemed infant communion necessary to salvation, and Trent's evasions here were intolerable.   But 'as there is no prohibition of it, so no command for it.'   Examination was commanded only of those who needed it, 'and infants, without examination, can as well receive the effect of the eucharist, as, without repentance, they can have the effect of baptism.'   Declaring the Lord's death 'is done by the action of every one that communicates', while the discerning the Lord's body was not required of them, 'for till they can do evil, they cannot be tied to do good.'   Yet John 6 was not a directly sacramental discourse and 'The thing itself, then, being left in the midst and undetermined, it is in the power of the church to give it, or to deny it.'

In favour of infant admission Taylor gave twelve reasons:
　　'The sacraments of the gospel are the great channels of the grace of God.'
　　'This grace always descends upon them that that do not hinder it.'
　　None can deny with certainty that infants receiving communion would also receive its fruits.

---

[47]　J.Taylor, *The Liberty of Prophesying* v in R.Heber (ed) *Works*, rev C.P. Eden (London, 1847-54) v.432f.
[48]　*ibid.* xviii, *ed.cit.* pp.547f, 575-77.
[49]　J.Taylor, *The Life of Christ* I.9.vi.34, *ibid* ii.275f.
[50]　J.Taylor, *The Life of Christ* III.15.xix.15, *ibid* ii.652f.

There are many acts of predisposition required equally for baptism, but the church does not consider children obliged to these.

What is done on our part obliges us only when we can understand, but what is done on God's part is always ready to those who can receive it.

Infants cannot come alone to Christ, but 'the Church, their mother, can bring them.'

'They who are capable of the grace of the sacrament may also receive its sign.'

'The same grace, being conveyed to them in one sacrament, may also be imparted to them in the other.'

'As they can be born again, without their own consent', so they can be fed by others.

If communion is denied, 'a gap be opened upon equal pretences' to deny baptism.

Infant participation in the passover pointed to infant participation in the supper.

It was first refused them 'when the doctrine of transubstantiation entered.'

But there were also arguments against infant communion:

Baptized infants are already admitted to the promises of the gospel.

Second graces are given for well using the first; the promises made in baptism must be personally accepted before any new grace can be sacramentally imparted.

Necessity, the motive for infant baptism, is lacking here.

Baptism is the sacrament of the new-born, while the eucharist is that of the perfect.

As Paul said, 'We have no such custom.'

In short, infant communion was lawful but not necessary, hence 'the present practice of the church is to be our rule and measure of peace, and determination of the article.'[51]

Herbert Thorndike denied that infant communion had been deemed necessary for salvation and argued that Innocent and Augustine referred to eating and drinking through baptism.[52] But 'the eucharist being nothing but the confirming and seconding of the covenant of baptism, the reason

[51] J.Taylor, *The Worthy Communicant* III.2, *ibid* viii.89-94.
[52] H.Thorndike, *Epilogue* 1.23 in *Works* (Oxford, 1844-54) ii.453-58.

why they were baptized inferred the giving of them the eucharist.' Infant communion might not be expedient but it was neither unlawful nor a profanation. Infants could not examine themselves, but nor could they be taught as soon as they were baptized, and 'if the Church duly presume, that with remission of sins they attain the gift of God's Spirit by being baptized; did it unduly presume, that ... the gift of the Holy Ghost may be strengthened by receiving the eucharist?' But he concluded with Taylor that 'he that contents himself with the practice of the church for unity's sake will prove the best Christian.'[53]

Patristic editors like Stephen Baluz[54] and liturgiologists like John Bona[55] now began to study infant communion more critically, and in 1673 a Lutheran, J.F. Mayer, published a treatise of 15,000 words.[56] He noted the early evidence for infant communion and argued that it had been given in both kinds.[57] He denied that it was an apostolic custom[58] and saw its origin in the 'otiose' sacramental interpretation of John 6.[59] Finally he referred to the Bohemians, criticized Trent, cited Musculus as the only reformer to defend it and summarized the arguments of Quenstedt for opposing it.[60] He provided a rich mine of patristic, scholastic and reformation references, but his work was marred by his concern to lambast the Romans.

From the Roman side Jacques Bossuet reached much the same conclusion as Taylor. The church had always believed 'that infants are capable to receive the Eucharist as well as Baptism, and finds no more obstacle, as to communion, in these words of St Paul, "Let a man examine himself and so let him eat", than she finds, as to Baptism, in these words of our Saviour, "Teach and Baptize".' But the eucharist could not be absolutely necessary to infants who had received remission of sins in baptism, hence 'it is a matter of discipline to give or not to give them communion at that age.' For good reasons the church had given it to them for eleven or twelve

---

[53]   *ibid* III.8.27 in *Works* iv.182f
[54]   S.Baluz, 'Notes' on Cyprian's *De Haereticorum Baptismate* (PL 3.1079f) and on Regino's *De Ecclesiasticis Disciplinis* (PL 132:419f)
[55]   J.Bona, *Rerum Liturgicarum* (Rome, 1671) bk 2 ch 19, pp.451-55.
[56]   J.F.Mayer, *Commentarius Historico-Theologicus de Eucharistia Infantibus olim Data* (First edition, Leipzig, 1673; second edition, Jena, 1734).
[57]   *id.* pp.5-33.
[58]   *id.* pp.34-42
[59]   *id.* pp.42-47.
[60]   *id.*pp.47-62.

hundred years, but for other good reasons she had later ceased to give it to them.[61]

Several writers still noted the eastern practice[62], and Thomas Smith was adamant that they communicated infants in both kinds.[63]   The reformed Johann Suicer[64] and the Benedictine Edmond Martene[65] continued Bona's liturgical researches, while Joseph Bingham criticized his defence of Trent, and repeated Hospinian's objections.[66]   Meanwhile William Wall argued that infant communion was not as old as infant baptism.   Cyprian showed only that 'children of four or five' received it in his particular church, and it was first given to infants in the time of Innocent and Augustine.   It was then adopted by the Greek church, 'which was then low in the world' and followed the example of Rome.   It was dropped by Rome when she accepted transubstantiation, but it continued among the Greeks who did not accept this.   Anabaptists argued that the fathers' testimony to infant baptism was weakened by their testimony to infant communion, but the grounds of the two practices were different.   John 6 did not apply to sacramental eating as John 3 applied to baptism. Circumcision was given to infants, but the passover not 'to the youngest infants'.   Baptism was 'an initiating or entering sacrament. The eucharist not so', and there was express scriptural command (Deuteronomy 29.10-12) for infants to be initiated into the covenant.   However, baptists could not argue both that infant baptism was 'a new thing' and that infant communion had been practised by the fathers.[67]

[61]   J.Bossuet, *Traité de la Communion sous les deux Espèces* (Brussells, 1682) pt 1 sec 3 pp.39-57, esp p.53.   (ET, Paris, 1685) pp 65-94, esp 88f.

[62]   P Vansleb, *Histoire de l'église d'Alexandrie* (Paris, 1677) pt.2 ch.21 pp.80-82, ch.24 p.85f; pt.3 ch.2 p.206; Paul Ricaut, *The Present State of the Greek and Armenian Churches* (London, 1679) pt.2 ch.8 pp.432f; Faustus Naironus, *Euoplia Fidei Catholicae Romanae* (Rome, 1694), pp 127f, 131f; Eusebe Renaudot, *Liturgicarum Orientalium Collectio* (1716), second edn (Frankfurt, 1847), i.270f.

[63]   T.Smith, *An Account of the Greek Church*, (London 1680) pp.161f, and – fuller, and referring to correspondence with Archbishop Joseph Georgirenes - 'Praemonitio ad lectorem de infantum communione apud Graecos' in *Miscellanea* (London, 1686).   I am grateful to Michael E Martin for introducing me to his essay, 'Some western images of Athos in early modern times, c. 1554-1678' in *Byzantine and Modern Studies*, XXII (1998) pp.51-74 which includes on p.72f a previously unpublished letter on the subject from Georgirenes to Smith.

[64]   J.Suicer, *Thesaurus Ecclesiasticus* (Amsterdam 1682); second edn (Amsterdam, 1728) ii.1136-39.

[65]   E.Martene, *De Antiquis Ecclesiae Ritibus* (Rouen 1700-02); second edn (ch 1 art 15 sec 11-15) (Antwerp, 1736) i.152-55.

[66]   J.Bingham, *The Antiquities of the Christian Church* XII.i.3, XIV.iv.7, XV.vii.4, (Bohn (ed), London, 1850) i.545, ii.797-800, 829f.

[67]   H.Cotton (ed), William Wall, *The History of Infant Baptism* (Oxford, 1835) 9:15-17, ii.178-95, cf also ii.503.

Wall's interpretation of Cyprian, as of the rise of the practice among the Greeks, was bizarre, and John Gale replied that Cyprian spoke as convincingly of infant communion as of infant baptism, and that infant communion had invariably followed infant baptism.[68] William Whiston argued that all ancient authors attested that the baptized were admitted immediately to the supper and that Justin's statement that 'it is not lawful for any to partake of the Eucharist but such as believe the things we teach' was 'a strong testimony' against the admission of infants to either sacrament. But from Cyprian onwards infants had been admitted to both on the ground of absolute necessity, and 'This Admission of Uncatechetized and Incapable Infants so contrary to the original Instituting, has been one great occasion of the Formality, Disorders and Wickedness of all the later Ages.'[69] Wall's reply to his critics simply restated his earlier arguments.[70]

In 1728 there was published posthumously *An Essay in Favour of the Ancient Practice of Giving the Eucharist to Children* by James Peirce, a Presbyterian who had been excluded for arianism. Peirce stated that his sympathy for infant communion had met 'contempt, horror and detestation' and he wrote 'by way of inquiry rather than as a peremptory determination'. If he was right, others would perceive this, and in any event he would 'rest satisfied in having discharg'd a good conscience'. But he hoped that those who thought him wrong about 'very little children' would consider whether their arguments would hold against 'those of six or seven years old'; he had met several who disagreed with the former but could contemplate the latter.[71]

Working backwards, Peirce argued that infant communion had continued in Bohemia until the eve of the Reformation[72], that it had been abandoned elsewhere in the west only when gross corruptions were introduced[73], and that it was 'a considerable oversight in the first reformers in general, that they seem hardly to have allow'd the least consideration' to it.[74]

---

[68] J.Gale, 'Reflections on Mr Wall's Account of Infant Baptism, 1711' in H. Cotton, *ed.cit.* iii.554, 573.

[69] W.Whiston, *Primitive Infant-Baptism Revived* (London,1712) pp.12, 31, 34, 40, 47. For Justin, cf *Apologia* i.66 (A.W. Blunt (ed), Cambridge University Press, Cambridge, 1911) p.98.

[70] Wall, 'A Defence of *The History of Infant Baptism,* 1720' in H. Cotton, *ed.cit.* iv.44f, 436f

[71] J.Peirce, *An Essay in Favour of the Ancient Practice of Giving the Eucharist to Children,* Preface pp.iii-vii.

[72] *id.* pp.5-8.

[73] *id.* pp.8-19.

[74] *id.* p.18.

Augustine described it as apostolic, it was the custom in Cyprian's time, and there was no reason to believe it peculiar to Carthage. There was no specific mention before Cyprian, but no one could point to its novel introduction or to any dispute in connection with it. No primitive doctrine argued against it, and there was no class of 'baptized catechumens'. The primitive attitude to the elements as the food of immortality and the eucharistic interpretation of John 6 both made it likely that infants were communicated.[75] In short, 'Tis highly probable that this had been the practice of the Christian church even from the apostles days.'[76]

This conclusion could stand only if infant communion accorded with scripture, and Peirce now sought to demonstrate this:

'The baptism and communion of infants stand upon the same foot.' They are members of the visible church; they have an interest in the new covenant; they are capable of salvation; they may be devoted to God; they can be brought to Christ; they are disciples, to be taught to observe all his commands of which this is one.

The action can be performed as well when infants receive as when they do not. His body was broken, and his blood shed, for them, and if they can partake of the benefits of the sacrifice they can partake of the sacrificial bread.

'The right of infants to communicate' may be argued from 1 Corinthians 10.16. They have 'interest and part' in his body and blood, and the signs of this communion belong to them.

Without infants 'the Lord's Supper will not signify the unity of Christ's mystical body, and so will not answer one great end and design of the institution.'

In 1 Corinthians 12.12f 'Paul proves that all Christians are one by their all partaking of one cup.'

If the Corinthians ate their ordinary meal in the assembly they probably had their families with them, hence it is 'highly probable' that children were admitted there.

---

[75] *id.* pp.19-53.
[76] *id.* pp.53-75.

Infants have the right 'from the nature of the ordinance' as a badge of the people of God. If they partook of Gentile tables, they can partake of the Lord's table.

Infants had the right 'to partake of the sacraments of the old testament', and they surely enjoy a similar right to the sacraments of the new testament.

'Baptized infants may be admitted to communion with the church in prayers; and therefore they may in the Lord's Supper.'

'Children are capable of what may well be thought sufficient to qualify them to receive.' If they are not able to take and eat, they can at least drink.[77]

Peirce next considered the objections. Infants could not remember, examine themselves, discern the Lord's body or show forth his death, but nor could they repent and believe before baptism. The primary remembrance, to put God in remembrance of the sacrifice of his Son, was made on behalf of the whole church, infants as well as adults. The examination did not concern infants, while discerning the body referred to the confusion between a sacred and a common meal. The showing forth of the Lord's death was accomplished by the actions, not by the recipients' sentiments. If infants' participation would reduce the solemnity of the sacrament or imply an *ex opere operato* view, this would apply equally to their baptism. That the supper was to confirm grace and not to initiate it was not a scriptural distinction; saving grace could be bestowed at the supper, and in any case antecedent grace had been received at baptism.[78]

Lastly Peirce listed the advantages of a revival of infant communion. It would give greater consistency to the argument for infant baptism. It would ease the scruples of pious souls who saw the supper as a privilege beyond the ordinary Christian. Communions would be better attended, and the sacrament administered more regularly. It would make good impressions on children, and bring them more under spiritual discipline instead of being left to shift for themselves after baptism. It would give church governors greater advantage in dealing with parents, and would make parents and masters more careful. The greater numbers would lead to more orderly discipline, and it might well contribute to a healing of divisions.[79]

[77]   *id.* pp.76-146.
[78]   *id.* pp.147-70.
[79]   *id.* pp.171-83.

Peirce's historical reconstruction was a bold one, but his scriptural justification and his answers to objections represent as strong a statement for infant communion as has ever been made and much of his exegesis still stands. But he expected to be opposed, and he was. In 1736 a Lutheran, Peter Zorn, dissatisfied with Mayer, published in Berlin a much lengthier *Historia Eucharistiae Infantium*. He accepted that infant communion was as old as Cyprian, but denied that it was apostolic.[80] He saw it as based on the notion of necessity derived from John 6[81], and he lamented the ignorance of Trent's assessment of the fathers.[82] It declined as a result of transubstantiation[83], and Rome's subsequent refusal of infants represented a change of doctrine not just of practice.[84] Having referred to the Bohemians[85] he then turned to the Greeks. He found fewer early references here, but noted that they now deemed it necessary.[86] He next considered Roman, Reformed and Lutheran writers[87], and after noting miscellaneous references[88] he finally looked at Peirce. When he began his work he had not seen this, but a synopsis had now reached him and he was unconvinced both by Peirce's 'argument from silence' and by his replies to the objections, 'Peirce thinks that he is refuting his opponents' arguments admirably, but men of sound judgement will not accept this.'[89]

With immense learning Zorn considered all relevant patristic passages and quoted scores of later writers. But he offered, as his title implied, a *history* of infant communion. His work was primarily a discussion of what others had said, his biblical and doctrinal treatment was slight, and he had nothing like the originality or clarity of Peirce. There soon followed a more deliberate reply to Peirce. In *A Review of the Doctrine of the Eucharist* in 1737, Daniel Waterland recognized that Peirce had offered 'suggestions which bear a plausible appearance', but initially he was content to follow Wall in ascribing infant communion to the sacramental interpretation of John 6 at the start of the fifth century.[90]

[80]   P.Zorn, *Historia Eucharistiae Infantium* (Berlin, 1736) pp.89-105.
[81]   *id.* pp.116-36.
[82]   *id.* pp.136-58.
[83]   *id.* pp.158-70.
[84]   *id.* pp.170-79.
[85]   *id.* pp.179-92.
[86]   *id.* pp.202-318.
[87]   *id.* pp.394-458.
[88]   *id.* pp.459-521.
[89]   *id.* pp.521-48.
[90]   D.Waterland, *A Review of the Doctrine of the Eucharist* in W. Van Mildert (ed) *Works* (Oxford, 1843) iv.563.

Between the writing of the *Review* and its publication, however, he revised his opinion and concluded that communicating children at ten, seven or even earlier was ancient and perhaps general, but communicating infants as a necessity on the basis of John 6 did not start before the eighth or ninth century, was never general, and in the west where it began was short-lived.[91]

Waterland explained his revised opinion in *An Inquiry concerning the Antiquity of the Practice of Infant Communion, as founded on the notion of its Strict Necessity*, published posthumously in 1742[92], with a preface by Joseph Clarke summarizing the work of earlier writers.[93]   He saw Cyprian as referring to children not infants and as based on expediency not necessity, and he dismissed the argument that Augustine provided 'uncontestable evidences' of infant communion on the ground of strict necessity because it contradicted his doctrine of 'the complete sufficiency of Baptism'.[94]   He could not consistently have taught the necessity of infant communion, and he did not interpret John 6 of the outward sacrament.   Even his explicit references to infants partaking of the Lord's body and blood and of the table did not apply to the eucharist over and above baptism,

> 'They are actually, not literally, communicants: they have not eaten the eucharistical bread, nor drunk the consecrated wine: very true; but yet they are partakers of the spiritual feast, and have a part in the mystical banquet; and therefore are, in effect, and in just construction of Gospel-law, companions at the Lord's table.   They are *fideles*, that is, communicants, in just account ...and therefore virtually, or interpretatively, partakers of the altar. ... Baptized infants, during their minority, are communicants in right, as true Christians, and as denizens of the city of God; and they are also communicants in effect, and in real enjoyment, as really partaking of the Christian banquet.'[95]

Waterland's exegesis of Augustine's baptismal theology is convincing and it is unlikely that, despite his ambiguities, Augustine taught the strict necessity of infant communion.   But Waterland was reading Cyprian and later writers with the unwarranted assumption that there *must* have been a

---

[91]   *id*. iv.460.
[92]   *An Inquiry*, vi.39-72.
[93]   *id*. v.398-415.
[94]   *id*. vi.43.
[95]   *id*. vi.46-53.

minimum age 'which the wisdom and integrity of church governors can determine.'[96]   He never seems to have considered that if infants were communicants 'in effect' in the strong sense which he claimed, they might also have been literal communicants.

Meanwhile, infant communion had now been revived by the Usagers, a small group of nonjurors who wished to restore certain primitive usages, and in 1734 Thomas Deacon, one of their bishops, published *A Complete Collection of Devotions*.   As W.J. Grisbrooke explained, 'Years before, the Usagers' opponents had warned them that once a return was made to *some* primitive customs, others would follow, until Communion would be given to infants', and Deacon's work was 'the fulfilment of their warning prophecy.'[97]   In Deacon's actual liturgy, the deacon gives the order, based on *Apostolic Constitutions* VIII, 'Mothers, take care of your children', and children are mentioned again in a rubric about the administration.[98]

In 1747 Deacon expounded his position in *A Full, True and Comprehensive View of Christianity*.   In his shorter catechism he explained that baptized infants must receive the eucharist 'because our Saviour's command is universal' and 'because the Eucharist is necessary to continue this Divine Spirit in them, to make them one body with Christ, and to render their bodies incorruptible.'[99]   In his longer catechism he sought to produce scriptural arguments in favour, to confirm it by the tradition of the church, to answer the usual objections and to repeat the advantages.   As against Peirce, he worked from scripture rather than back to it, but his fifty closely-printed pages are largely a repetition of Peirce, sometimes even *verbatim*.   He expanded on Peirce only in his treatment of Augustine where he stated that Augustine's arguments for infant communion were 'so full, clear and strong that one would think it impossible to avoid the force of them.'   With a thinly veiled reference to Waterland he continued,

> 'Yet some persons of sense and learning, being hard put to it to justify their own practice, have invented a subtle evasion, which is, that though S Augustine maintained the necessity of infants partaking of Christ's body and blood yet that they are in effect by

---

[96]   *id*. vi.69.
[97]   W.Jardine Grisbrooke (ed), *Anglican Liturgies of the Seventeenth and Eighteenth Centuries* (Alcuin Club Collections XL, SPCK, London, 1958) pp.117f.
[98]   *id*. pp.303, 314.
[99]   T.Deacon, *A Full, True and Comprehensive View of Christianity:* 'Shorter Catechism: Lesson xxix' pp.78f.

baptism made partakers of the same, for that they are exhibited spiritually in Baptism as well as the Eucharist.'[100]

Deacon's group was small and its influence negligible.   But there is a tantalizingly brief and ambiguous reference in a letter of John Wesley.   In 1748 the deist Conyers Middleton argued that eucharistic abuses had appeared very early: 'This Sacrament was administered likewise, in all their public communions, to infants, even of the tenderest age, before they were able to speak: and was constantly styled "the sacrifice of the Body of Christ".'[101]   But Wesley challenged Middleton: 'That "in Tertullian's days it [the bread] was carried home and locked up as a divine treasure" I call upon you to prove; as also that infant communion was an abuse or the styling it "the sacrifice of the body of Christ".'[102]   This is best taken as indicating that Wesley was not convinced that infant communion was an abuse[103], though it can also be taken as denying that such an abuse as he would have agreed it to be actually existed then.[104]

---

[100]   *id.* Lessons 113-36, pp.343-393, esp pp.367f.
[101]   C.Middleton, *A Free Inquiry into the Miraculous Powers which are supposed to have subsisted in the Christian Church* (London, 1749) pp.57ff.
[102]   Letter of 4 January 1749 in J.Telford (ed), *Standard Letters of John Wesley* (Epworth Press, London, 1931) ii.320.
[103]   Cf H. Holloway, *The Confirmation and Communion of Infants and Young Children* (Skeffington, London, 1901) title-page.
[104]   John C Bowmer, who kindly located this quotation for me, described it in his letter as 'one of those quotations which ought to be used only in its context', and I suspect he took the latter interpretation.

3. Marking Time

For the next hundred years infant communion was of only antiquarian concern.[105] The Oxford Movement led to a renewed interest, but so slowly that the historian W.E.H. Lecky thought it curious that 'those very noisy contemporary divines ...have left unpractised what was undoubtedly one of the most universal, and was believed to be one of the most important, of the institutions of early Christianity.'[106]

Contact with the east provided the initial stimulus. William Palmer of Oxford met the Russian, A.S. Khomiakoff, who wrote c.1850 that in baptizing, confirming and communicating infants the church was acting in the spirit of love 'in order that the first thought of a child arriving at years of discretion should be not only a desire, but also a joy for sacraments which have been already received.' Those who deprived children of these did not comprehend the majesty of God's sacraments, and subjected doctrine to scholastical explications.[107] At the same time J.M. Neale described the west's disuse of the primitive custom as 'a great abuse' and 'a gross corruption', and thought it 'strange that the Greeks have not made it a more prominent subject of complaint.'[108] W.E. Scuddamore saw 'no reason' why children should not be admitted 'at a very early age' since grace 'can work effectually in the soul even of unconscious infants', and 'Infant Communion was, in fact the rule of the early Church.'[109] Infant communion is said[110] to have been urged also by F.W. Puller. However, it was only the small Catholic Apostolic church which in the nineteenth century attempted even a modest revival.[111]

[105] Cf Odoricus Raynaldus, *Annales Ecclesiastici* 8.1421.l2 (Lucca, 1752) p.534; A.A. Pelliccia, *The Polity of the Christian Church*, 1779 (ET J.C. Bennett , London, 1883) pp.18f.

[106] W.E.H.Lecky, *History of European Morals* ii.4 (London, 1869) p.6.

[107] ET in W.J. Birkbeck (ed), *Russia and the English Church during the last fifty years* (London, 1895) p.215.

[108] J.M.Neale, *A History of the Holy Eastern Church* (London, 1850) pt 1, ii.999-1001.

[109] W.E.Scuddamore, *Notitia Eucharistia*, second edn (London, 1876) pp.53-55; cf also entry on 'Infant Communion' in W.Smith and S. Cheetham, *Dictionary of Christian Antiquities* (London, 1875-80) i.835-37

[110] Cf K.D. Mackenzie, 'The Relation of Confirmation to Baptism' in *Confirmation*, by various writers (SPCK, London,1926) i.287. But Mackenzie gives no reference here, though Puller certainly advocated infant confirmation in *What is the Distinctive Grace of Confirmation?* (London, 1880) pp.36f.

[111] E. Miller, *The History and Doctrines of Irvingism* (London, 1878) ii.71, explained that infants were first communicated, once, at about the age of two. When eight or nine they communicated on the four great feasts, but they became regular communicants only around fourteen. Cf also K.W. Stevenson, 'A Theological Reflection on the Experience of Inclusion/ Exclusion at the Eucharist', originally published in the *Anglican Theological Review* LXVIII (1986) pp.212-21 and reprinted in Ruth A. Meyers (ed), *op.cit*, pp.42-56.

Meanwhile opponents and supporters pleaded for consistency. In 1864 C. H. Spurgeon, rejecting the relevance of Mark 10.13-16, argued 'if an infant has a right to baptism, it has a right to come to the Lord's Table.'[112] Conversely in 1899 Charles E. Jefferson, an American Congregationalist, asked, 'If we baptize our children, why have they not a right to the Supper of the Lord?' How could they have a right to the symbol of his cleansing power but not to that of his sustaining grace? If baptism went by households, so too should the eucharist.[113]

A new phase began in 1901 when Henry Holloway urged *The Confirmation and Communion of Infants and Young Children.* In a preface Lord Halifax criticized the scholastic rejection of primitive practice[114], and Holloway noted that the only prayer-book hindrances were the rubric requiring confirmation before communion and the preface restricting this to the instructed. For neither of these could he find authority in scripture.[115] The catechism spoke of baptism and communion alike as 'generally necessary to salvation'[116], and the 'evil, rationalist notion' that an intelligent reception' was necessary for children 'has perhaps done more mischief to religion than all the other errors of Popery put together.'[117] East and west had communicated 'unconscious infants ...from very early times indeed, if not from the days of the apostles.'[118] The onus of proof lay with those who dispensed with the primitive practice. If infants were denied 'it must be on the same authority as adults are enjoined to receive', i.e. the words of Christ and the apostles[119], but, as Peirce had shown, the evidence of scripture was in favour. The subject was treated again by Darwell Stone. In 1899 he expressed the hope that the church would 'restore the primitive custom of administering Confirmation and First Communion, in the case both of infants and of adults, immediately after Baptism'[120], and in 1904 he gave his reasons for this. The catechism saw the supper, like baptism, as 'generally necessary to salvation'. Western theology distinguished between the necessity of 'means' and of 'precept' and attached only the latter to the eucharist, yet

---

[112] C.H.Spurgeon, 'Children Brought to Christ, Not to the Font' in *The Metropolitan Pulpit*, no 581, London X (1864) p.415.

[113] C.E.Jefferson, 'Work among Young People' in E.C. Webster (ed), *Volume of Proceedings of the Second International Congregational Council ... 1899* (Boston, Mass, 1900) pp.307-13.

[114] Lord Halifax 'Preface' in H. Holloway, *The Confirmation and Communion of Infants and Young Children*, pp. xvii-xx.

[115] *id.* pp.4f.

[116] *id.* p.11.

[117] *id.* p.16.

[118] *id.* p.58.

[119] *id.* p.98.

[120] Darwell Stone, *Holy Baptism* (Longmans Green, London, 1899) p.186.

'The moral law of God appears to require that what is necessary to salvation because of a command is necessary also for some deeper underlying reason', and the words in John 6 were exactly parallel to those in John 3. The early church administered communion 'without restriction as to age', and 'Whatever reasons are afforded ... for the Baptism of infants apply also to the Communion of infants.' Baptized children who through no fault of their own died without communion were granted some compensatory grace, but 'that consideration does not remove the fear of the loss to spiritual life which may have resulted from the withholding of Communion, through century after century, from babes and young children'. Moreover 'the unconscious infant and the growing child would not necessarily be more irreverent than many adults.'[121]

In 1910 Rome's *Quam Singulari* recognized that 'from its very earliest beginnings' the church had admitted little children, but it still upheld the Lateran decree that they should be admitted 'only when they had a certain use of dawning reason'.[122] Henry Leclercq now summarized the general historical evidence[123], but inevitably *Quam Singulari* stimulated further studies. Jules Besson, L Andrieux and J Baumgartler[124] wrote on the age of first communion, P Browe[125] explored medieval practice, and Maurice de la Taille even claimed 'a necessity of means' for the eucharist. The fathers had attested infant communion and, though Trent had denied any absolute necessity for physical reception, it was still 'absolutely necessary at least by desire', and baptism could be defined as the sacrament of the 'communion of desire' which 'as soon as received, initiates the recipient to the fruits of the Eucharist.'[126] On actual communion, however, the Roman position was clear. As Besson declared, 'A child is *capable* of Communion once it is baptized; it is bound to communicate once it has discretion. Between these two limits it belongs to the Church to decide.'[127]

---

[121] Darwell Stone, *The Holy Communion* (Longmans Green, London, 1904) pp.188-200, also pp.303f.

[122] H. Denzinger and A. Schonmetzer (eds), *Enchiridion Symbolorum Definitionum et Declarationum,* 32nd edn, (Barcelona, 1963) nos 3530-32, p.687. The decree was incorporated in the 1917 canon law, *Codex Iuris Canonici* 88, 854, 859, 906 (Westminster, Maryland, 1949) pp.19, 286-88, 304; cf also J.A. Jungmann, *Handing on the Faith* (Herder, London, 1959) pp.290-300.

[123] H.Leclercq, *Dictionnaire d'Archéologie Chrétienne et de Liturgie* (Paris, 1914) 6:2440-45

[124] Jules Besson, *L'Age de la Première Communion* (Tournai, 1911); L. Andrieux, *La Première Communion: Histoire et Discipline* (Paris, 1911), J. Baumgartler, *Die Erstkommunion der Kinder* (Kosel and Pustet, Munich, 1929). I have not had access to these studies.

[125] P.Browe, 'Die kinderkommunion im Mittelalter'in *Scholastik* V (1930) 1-45; *Die Pflichtkommunion im Mittelalter* (Munich, 1940).

[126] M. de la Taille, *Mysterium Fidei* (Paris, 1921) thesis 46, pp.568f, and thesis 49 pp.587-600; also 'An Outline of the Mystery of Faith' in *The Mystery of Faith and Human Opinion Contrasted and Defined*, ET (Sheed and Ward, London, 1934) pp.30-32.

[127] J.Besson, *op.cit.*, p.24, cited F.M. De Zulueta, *Early First Communion* (1911) p.18.

In 1943 Helle Georgiadis drew further attention to the east when he contrasted his two childhood experiences. At an Anglican eucharist children were taken out early, but at the Orthodox service there were many children and babes:

> 'A child of Orthodox parents will be brought up in the Church, whereas in the West, the child will be trained by the Church, his parents, and possibly his school, to bring him to a point of readiness necessary before the Church can accept him as a full member.'

The Orthodox child had a recognized status in the church from birth: 'He is never looked on either as a sinful little alien to be "saved" or something preciously individual to be left to his own conscience', he 'can never remember the time when his parents attended Holy Communion without him; he was never told that the service was too long for him or taken out before the sermon, which was "only for grown-ups".' With the Orthodox service having 'no definite beginning or end' his parents would probably not have attended the whole service, yet 'because the people did not follow the service from a book, the child can never remember the time when inability to read fluently made it impossible for him to hold his own with the people around him.' In Orthodoxy, 'the transition from babyhood to adulthood is so smooth that the child accepts his Church membership as naturally as he accepts his family relationships. But in the West, Church membership carries with it certain tests which he must work for and pass.'[128]

Eastern practice was commended again when Herbert Pakenham-Walsh described the infant communion practised by the Syrian church in his Ashram and claimed, 'All that can be urged theologically in favour of Infant Baptism can be urged in favour of Infant Communion.' Pakenham-Walsh was cited approvingly by A.R. Vidler who added, 'We do not see how it is that, if infants may rightly be baptized, they may rightly be deprived of holy communion.'[129]

By now Karl Barth, opposing infant baptism, had observed that if it were defended as illustrating antecedent grace, 'a claim might be put forward for the admission of infants to the Lord's Supper. Indeed, since by reason of their baptism they are members of the church, properly speaking this must be claimed.'[130] Oscar Cullmann replied that the eucharist was

[128] H.Georgiadis, 'Christian Upbringing in East and West'in *Sobernost*, NS no.27 (June 1943) pp.19-22.
[129] H.Pakenham-Walsh, 'Treasures of Devotion from the Syrian Liturgy of Malabar'in *Star of the East* (December 1944) cited by A.R. Vidler in *Theology* XLVIII (1945) p.193.
[130] K.Barth, *The Teaching of the Church regarding Baptism* (1943; ET, SCM, London, 1948) p.62.

distinguished from baptism first by its repetition and secondly because here the death and resurrection of Jesus were related to the community rather than to the individual. At baptism the individual was set once for all at the point where salvation operates, i.e. within the church, but at the eucharist 'there gather, to the exclusion of the unbelieving and the not-yet-believing, those who already believe and who again and again assure themselves of their salvation as a community.'[131] P.C. Marcel in another reply affirmed that scripture assigned to the children of believers the same privileges as those who were of an age to confess their faith.[132] The English Baptist, H.H. Rowley, seized on this and urged that if infant baptism had scriptural warrant without any specific injunction, 'the corollary should be accepted that the Lord's Supper should equally be administered to children.'[133]

Another response to Barth was made by John Murray. If paedobaptists were inconsistent, 'far less would be at stake in admitting infants to the Lord's supper than would be at stake in abandoning infant baptism.' But in fact there were sufficient distinctions between baptism and the supper to make it reasonable 'that the one should be dispensed to infants and the other not'. Baptism signified and sealed what lay at the basis of a state of salvation; the supper signified something consequent upon it. The union with Christ and cleansing signified by baptism did not necessarily involve intelligent understanding, whereas the commemoration and communion signified by the supper involved recognition and conscious intelligent understanding. Baptism represented something performed once for all; the supper represented what was daily repeated. In baptism the water was appropriate to the infant; in the supper the bread and wine were not.[134]

In 1955 a Church of Scotland *Interim Report of the Special Commission on Baptism* claimed that while 'infant incorporation into the Body of Christ' seemed logically to demand their participation in the Supper, there was 'a fundamental difference' here,

'In Holy Baptism we are baptized by another, for it is the Sacrament of an act done upon us "as little children", but in the Lord's Supper

[131] O.Cullmann, *Baptism in the New Testament* (ET, SCM, London,1950) pp.29f. For a criticism of Cullman, cf G. Wainwright, *Christian Initiation* (Lutterworth, London 1969) p.28.

[132] P.C.Marcel, *The Biblical Doctrine of Infant Baptism* (ET, James Clarke, Cambridge, 1953) pp.123, 190.

[133] H.H.Rowley, 'Marcel on Infant Baptism' in *Expository Times* LXIV (1953) pp.361-63.

[134] J.Murray, *Christian Baptism* (Presbyterian and Reformed Publishing Company, Philadelphia, 1952) pp.77-79.

the command is: "This <u>do</u> in remembrance of Me". Certainly here too the primary fact is what God does, and not what we do, but clearly this involves an active participation and also a self-offering in the name of Christ which stands in marked contrast to Baptism which is not self-administered.'[135]

Critics saw this as 'one of the lamest sections' of the report. The emphasis on active participation was negated by the admission that even in the Supper the primary fact is what God does, and in any case the command was given not to isolated individuals but to a community which could 'do this' equally well with children present.[136] The commission implicitly admitted the weakness of its case three years later when it reduced the 'fundamental difference' to a difference 'that is fundamental for our practice' and a 'justification' of it[137], but, even as revised, the reasons for withholding communion from infants were later described as such as 'will hardly bear looking at'.[138]

Max Thurian of Taizé spoke of the abnormality of not admitting all the baptized but added 'Of course there is no question of ... children too young to be instructed enough to discern the Body of the Lord'.[139] But, as Geoffrey Wainwright noted, 'If faith is assumed to be present, whether actually, vicariously or proleptically, at the baptism of an infant, then similar assumptions are also applicable in the case of "discerning the body" at communion'.[140]

In the Church of England several reports contemplated earlier but never infant communion.[141] There was still wide sympathy for the traditional sequence of communion following confirmation; here, infant communion would have entailed infant confirmation, and for many this was

[135] Church of Scotland Commission, *Interim Report* (Edinburgh, 1955) p.28.
[136] J. Gray (ed), *Studies on Baptism* (Birmingham, nd, c.1959), p.11.
[137] Church of Scotland Commission, *The Biblical Doctrine of Baptism*, (St Andrew Press, Edinburgh, 1958), p.54.
[138] G. Wainwright, *op.cit* p.91 n.30. The Commission's history was weak, and John Heron, its joint convenor, was wrong by seven hundred years when he claimed that 'The Western Church, at least from the time of Augustine, has ... believed that infants should not be admitted to the Lord's table, because they are not yet able to examine themselves' ('Christian Initiation' in *Studia Liturgica* 1 (1962), p.44 and 'Baptism, Confirmation and the Eucharist' in B.S. Moss (ed), *Crisis for Baptism* (SCM, London, 1965) p.119).
[139] M.Thurian, *Consecration of the Layman*, 1957 (ET, Helicon, Dublin, 1963) pp.77f.
[140] G.Wainwright, *op.cit.* p.96 n.46.
[141] *Confirmation To-day* (Church Assembly, London, 1944); *The Theology of Christian Initiation* (SPCK, London, 1948); *Baptism and Confirmation Today* (SPCK, London, 1954)

inconceivable.   J.G. Davies argued for both[142], but G.W.H.Lampe questioned the necessity of the sequence.   He recognized pastoral arguments for admitting unconfirmed children but regarded the communion of unconscious children as 'quite indefensible', and 'quite contrary to the intention of the New Testament and the Fathers'.[143]   This, from an eminent biblical and patristic scholar, was an extraordinary statement.

---

[142] Contribution to discussion in Basil Minchin (ed), *Becoming a Christian*, (Faith Press, London, 1954) pp.71f.   Cf also his *The Spirit, The Church and the Sacraments* (Faith Press, London, 1954) p.194 and, later Massey H Shepherd, 1964 lecture printed in *Liturgy and Education* (Seabury, New York, 1965) pp.106f, cited by L.L. Mitchell, *Initiation and the Churches* (Pastoral Press, Washington DC, 1991) p.15 n.23.

[143] G.W.H.Lampe, 'Baptism and confirmation in the Light of the Fathers' in Basil Minchin, *op.cit* pp.46f.

4. The Last Fifty Years: (i) Theological Debate

In 1965 J.D.C.Fisher provided further light on the medieval decline of infant communion[144], in 1989 David R. Holeton published a major work on infant communion among the Hussites[145], and in 2003 I myself summarized the evidence from the New Testament to the Reformation.[146] Alongside these historical studies, there has been a debate much wider than anything in the past and also the first full-length advocacy since Peirce with Tim Gallant's 2002 *Feed My Lambs: Why the Lord's table should be restored to Covenant Children.*[147]

The debate had four particular stimulants. First, in 1960, came a strong repetition of the Baptist challenge by Paul K. Jewett in the United States. He contrasted the insistence on personal faith for communion with the dispensing of it for baptism, and stressed the weakness of attempts to divide the sacraments of 'initiating' and 'abiding', to make one passive and the other active and to demand actual remembrance in communion without actual faith at baptism.[148]

Second, in 1967, was a call by the first National Evangelical Anglican Congress at Keele for 'study as to whether the age of discretion is always the right time for admission', and the acknowledgement that 'Some of us would like the children of Christian families to be admitted as communicants at an early age.'[149]

Third, in 1975, there followed an essay, *Is the Lord's Supper for Children?*,

---

[144] J.D.C.Fisher, *Christian Initiation: Baptism in the Medieval West* (Alcuin Club Collection 47, SPCK, London, 1965). Cf also J.M.M. Dalby, 'The End of Infant Communion'in *Church Quarterly Review* CLXVII (1966) pp.59-71.

[145] D.R.Holeton, *La Communion des Tout-petits Enfants: Étude du Mouvement Eucharistique en Bohème vers la fin du Moyen-Age* (Bibliotheca 'Ephemerides Liturgicae' Subsidia 50, Centro Liturgico Vincenziano, Rome, 1989).

[146] Mark Dalby, *Infant Communion: The New Testament to the Reformation* (Alcuin/GROW Joint Liturgical Study 56, Grove Books, Cambridge)

[147] T.Gallant, *Feed My Lambs: Why the Lord's table should be restored to Covenant Children* (Pactum Reformanda, Grande Prairie, Alberta, Canada, 2002).

[148] Jewett's essay was first published in duplicated form in 1960 as *Infant Baptism and Confirmation*, then republished with minimal revisions as *Infant Baptism and the Covenant of Grace* (Eerdmans, Grand Rapids, Michigan, 1978), cf esp pp.41ff and 193-207.

[149] P.A.Crowe (ed), *Keele '67* (Falcon, London, 1967) para 74, p.35.

by Christian L. Keidel, an American Presbyterian who saw infant communion resting on three biblical truths: 'the analogy between the Lord's Supper and the Passover meal; the analogy between the Lord's Supper and other sacrificial meals in the old covenant; and finally, infant membership in the covenant'.[150]

Fourth, there developed an increasing tendency in many churches to make the eucharist the principal Sunday service. When non-sacramental worship was the norm, non-communicant children did not feel deprived, but, as many now regularly attended a eucharist where most adults communicated, some felt excluded, and often their parents were uneasy too.

There were also four principal arguments, though inevitably these overlap.

1. Infant Communion follows inevitably from their baptism or from their status within the covenant, and is a further witness to the priority of grace.

In 1965 the Swiss Reformed theologian, J.J. Von-Allmen, argued that communion is 'the inalienable right' of the baptized and, if we risked baptizing the children of Christian parents, 'we must also run the risk of permitting them to live on the spiritual food of the baptized'.[151] In 1966 J.A.T. Robinson claimed that communicant status was implied by membership: 'All things are yours because you are Christ's.' Admission to communion should be on the basis of baptism and chrysmation (administered together) and children could 'communicate with their parents when and as they are old enough to manage it physically'.[152] In 1967 Fisher asked 'if we justify infant Baptism on the ground that infants can receive the grace of Baptism proleptically, why cannot they also receive the grace of Confirmation and Communion proleptically?'[153] In 1968 Colin Buchanan, a prime mover at Keele, argued that the reformers were wrong to require 'all the right answers' before admission. Put simply, 'the

---

[150] C.L.Keidel, 'Is the Lord's Supper for Children?'in *Westminster Theological Journal*, Philadelphia, XXXVII (1975) pp.301-41; the quotation is from p.341. James B Jordan tells me that Keidel was influenced by Norman Shepherd, one of his teachers at Westminster Theological Seminary, and that infant communion had previously been advocated by Rousas John Rushdoony in *The Institutes of Biblical Law* (Craig Press, Nutley, New Jersey, 1973) pp.751-55.

[151] J.J.Von-Allmen, *Worship: Its Theology and Practice* (ET, Luttererworth, London, 1965) p.187.

[152] J.A.T.Robinson, 'Meeting, Membership and Ministry' in *Christian Freedom in a Permissive Society* (SCM, London, 1970) pp.162f (originally published in 1966 as *Prism Pamphlet* no.31). The biblical reference is 1 Corinthians 3.21f.

[153] J.D.C.Fisher, 'History and Theology' in M.C. Perry (ed), *Crisis for Confirmation* (SCM, London, 1967) pp.55f.

baptized person is a Christian, and the Christian is a communicant. Thus a baptized babe is in principle admissible to communion *with his parents'*, and the exact age was a matter for their discretion.[154] He noted later that 'if the parents themselves lapsed, then the children would be involved in lack of communion as well', though this was a practical observation rather than a theological one.[155]

Among Roman Catholics, in 1970 Charles Crawford asked why, if infants were baptized on 'the faith of the church', they could not receive communion on that basis.[156] In 1973 J.D. Crichton, stressed that 'it was the one mystery of Christ which we celebrate', and this might be sufficient reason to restore the baptismal communion of infants.[157] Robert W. Hovda added in 1976 that this 'would end the incongruous practice of baptizing someone and then immediately excommunicating him.'[158]

In the Church of Scotland, in 1977 James L. Weatherhead argued that 'Baptism is itself the evidence of faith necessary for admission to Communion ...We injure Baptism if we do not recognize that it confers an *unqualified* right to be admitted.'[159] In 1980 Finlay Macdonald claimed that there was no justification for withholding communion from baptized infants, and that 'the priority of grace' was one good reason for welcoming them.[160] In 1982 James B. Torrance argued that children belong to Christ by creation, redemption, and more particularly baptism, and from the very outset they should be made to feel that his table is for

---

[154] C.O.Buchanan , 'An Anglican Evangelical looks at Sacramental Initiation'in *Faith and Unity*, XII (1968) p.47.   Cf also C.O. Buchanan, J.I. Packer, E.L. Mascall and G. Leonard, *Growing into Union* (SPCK, London,1970) pp.60f and 66; and C.O Buchanan, *Baptismal Discipline* (Grove Booklets on Ministry and Worship 3, Grove Books, Bramcote, 1972) pp.9, 17; *A Case for Infant Baptism* (Grove Booklets on Ministry and Worship 20, Grove Books, Bramcote, 1973), 4th edn 1990, p.19 and rewritten edn 2009, p.16; *Children in Communion* (Grove Worship Series 112, Grove Books, Bramcote, 1990).

[155] C.O.Buchanan 'The Church and Baptism' in C.O. Buchanan (ed), *Evangelical Essays on Church and Sacraments* (SPCK, London, 1972) pp.60f; Cf also C.H. Hutchins, 'The Church and Holy Communion' in C.O. Buchanan (ed), *ibid*, p.72, and for further observations from Buchanan in his *Children in Communion* p.13.

[156] 'Infant Communion: Past Tradition and Present Practice' C.Crawford in *Theological Studies*, Baltimore, XXXI (1970) 524.

[157] C.Crawford, *Christian Celebration: The Sacraments* (Geoffrey Chapman, London, 1973) pp.34f.

[158] Robert W.Hovda, 'Hope for the Future: A Summary' in *Made, Not Born* (Murphy Center for Liturgical Research, University of Notre Dame, Notre Dame, Indiana, 1976) p.163.

[159] J.L.Weatherhead, 'Children in Worship with Special Reference to Holy Communion' in *Liturgical Review*, (Edinburgh, November 1977) p.10.

[160] Finlay Macdonald, 'Baptised Children, Confirmation and Holy Communion' in *Scottish Journal of Theology* XXXIII (1980) pp.551-65, esp 559f.   Cf also his 'Confirmation and Profession of Faith' in David G. Hamilton and Finlay A.J. Macdonald (eds), *Children at the Table* (Dept of Education, Church of Scotland, Edinburgh, 1982) pp.10-14.

them as well as for their parents. Additional demands can imply 'that you do not yet belong to Christ although you have been baptized' and 'can obscure the meaning of the Lord's Supper as a sacrament of the Gospel by making the offered grace conditional.'[161]

In America the debate now centred on the question of age.   In 1972 Urban T. Holmes favoured admission at three or four.[162]   Keidel stressed that he was advocating the communion only of those who were physically capable of eating.[163]   In 1976 a Lutheran, Eugene L Brand, saw no theological barrier to infant communion, though pastorally
> 'deferring full eucharistic participation until there is a dawning perception of life in community is possible.   Or there is a mediating compromise: administering the species to newly baptized infants in the baptismal eucharist, thus clearly demonstrating their right of access to the altar and completing the initiation rites in one motion, but then delaying the next communion for a few (very few!) years.'[164]

But in 1977 Holeton dismissed lowering the age as mere tinkering. Theologians could provide no rationale for initiation that did not include communicant status; social scientists could provide no particular rationale for ages like 5-8 years, and one either had to make communion the natural consequence of baptism or else push the age well into the teens.[165] In 1980 in England John M. Sutcliffe of the United Reformed Church, who had amassed evidence of the desire for communion of children some aged only 3-6 years, again saw no justification for a minimum age-limit.[166] In 1980 James F. White, an American Methodist, insisted that half-way or preparatory membership was 'a contradiction in terms', and that 'Those who have received baptism and the laying on of hands or anointing ought immediately to be welcomed to the Lord's table, no matter at what age they have come.[167]   In 1982 A.T. Eastman, an Episcopalian, urged similarly:

[161]   J.B.Torrance, 'Some Theological Grounds for Admitting Children to the Lord's Table' in David G. Hamilton and Finlay A.J. Macdonald (eds), op.cit. pp.5-7.
[162]   U.T.Holmes, Young Children and the Eucharist (Seabury Press, New York, 1972) pp.57-63.
[163]   C.L.Keidel, art.cit. pp.305f.
[164]   Eugene L.Brand, 'Baptism and Communion of Infants: A Lutheran View'in Worship (Collegeville, Minnesota) L (1976) pp.29-42.
[165]   David R.Holeton, 'Christian Initiation in some Anglican Provinces'in Studia Liturgica XII (1977) pp.146f. Cf also D. Stevick, Holy Baptism: Supplement to Prayer Book Studies 26 (Church Hymnal Corporation, New York, 1973), p.73, and Baptismal Moments; Baptismal Meanings (Church Hymnal Corporation, New York, 1987) pp.102ff.
[166]   John M.Sutcliffe, 'Children and Holy Communion', in G. Muller-Fahrenholz (ed), ... And do not hinder them, (WCC, Geneva, 1982) pp.24-36. This was a report of a WCC conference in 1980.
[167]   James F.White, Introduction to Christian Worship (Abingdon Press, Nashville 1980) p.201. Cf also his Sacraments as God's Self-Giving, (Abingdon Press, Nashville, 1983) pp.66f and 126.

'The newly-baptized, including infants, should *receive communion* to mark the completion of the threefold action of the rite. Parents may or may not wish to have their infants communicate regularly until somewhat later, but a crumb of bread and a drop of wine is easily and appropriately administered to them as an indication that they are full members of the Christian household.'[168]

In 1991 Glenn N. Davies in Australia stressed the 'activity' of the communicant and thought it was primarily for the parents to decide when an infant became a child.[169] James B. Jordan, an American covenant theologian, argued in 1992, 'When the child begins to drink from the cup at home, he should be given a cup at church. When he begins to chew teething biscuits at home, he can be given bread at church. Not before. Not later on.'[170] In 1993 Daniel Young deemed age-limits 'more and more anomalous': 'We must not fudge the principle: if we baptize infants we should be ready to communicate them.'[171]

Among Roman Catholics, in 1985 Gerard Austin argued that 'The title for admission to the Table of the Lord is far clearer through the sacraments of baptism and confirmation than through something as undetermined and nebulous as the age of discretion.' Where infant baptism persisted, 'infants should be baptized, confirmed and given first eucharist' at the same time.[172] In 1988 Aidan Kavanagh described initiation which did not end 'regularly and ordinarily in first communion' as 'severely abnormal, a *ritus interruptus*'. The logical conclusion of recent reforms was 'to confirm infants immediately after baptism and then to communicate them'.[173]

---

[168] A.T.Eastman, *The Baptizing Community* (Seabury Press, New York, 1982), p.81.

[169] Glenn N.Davies, 'The Lord's Supper for the Lord's Children' in *Reformed Theological Review* (Melbourne, L, 1991) p.12.

[170] J. B.Jordan, *A Letter on Paedocommunion, Rite Reasons* (Studies in Worship 21, 1992) p.2; cf also his *Swaddling Clothes and Paedocommunion, ibid* 78, 2001. In 1982 Jordan had published *Theses on Paedocommunion* (Geneva Papers, Geneva Divinity School, Tyler, Texas 1982), and in 1994 he issued four taped lectures on 'The Biblical Doctrine of Paedocommunion'. He has issued many more occasional contributions to the debate and these, along with his lectures, can be obtained from Biblical Horizons, PO Box 1096, Niceville, Florida, 32588-1096, USA.

[171] Daniel Young, *Welcoming Children to Communion* (Grove Worship Series 85, Grove Books, Bramcote, 1983) p.12. Cf also his comments, pp.16ff, on 'Can tiny children manage bread and wine?'

[172] Gerard Austin, *Anointing with the Spirit* (Pueblo, New York, 1985) pp.53f and 128-46.

[173] Aidan Kavanagh, *Confirmation: Origins and Reform* (Pueblo, New York, 1988) pp.88, 112f. For other Roman Catholic writers at this time, cf Kenan Osborne, *The Christian Sacraments of Initiation* (Paulist Press, New York, 1987) pp.70 and 151f, and Liam Walsh, *The Sacraments of Initiation* (Geoffrey Chapman, London, 1988) pp.159-63.

The most original argument came from John Pridmore in 1992. Infants are normally brought by their mother, but 'every time an expectant mother comes to communion she comes, quite literally, *carrying a child*. Her food is food for her unborn child. The child to be born, no less a child because yet unborn, is already receiving the body and blood of Christ.' Hence 'by administering the sacrament to the infant in his mother's arms we are simply continuing what we did when we gave the sacrament to the mother with the same infant in her womb ... We are not asking to lower the age limit but to abolish it.'[174]   Later, Gallant preferred to speak of 'children' rather than 'infants', though 'a child does not need to be very old to be physically capable of eating bread and drinking a bit of wine – just old enough to be off the breast.'[175]   Till then, 'in a real sense, when the nursing mother partakes, implicitly so does the child.'[176]

In the wider debate[177], Jordan saw nothing to suggest that baptized covenant children should undergo a further rite, catechizing, or an 'experience', before being eligible for the eucharist.[178]   In 1988 a Lutheran, H. Frederick Reisz jr, lamented that western practice represented 'a triumph of the rational and organizational over the doxological and theological', and insisted that the eucharist was for all the baptized, 'infants and children included, when and as they are able to receive'.[179] In the same year Robert S. Rayburn, a conservative Presbyterian, asked where scripture suggested that a participant in 'all the benefits of the covenant of grace' was to be denied their sign and seal; it was not clear why the word and one sacrament should be given to children but the Lord's supper not.[180]   In 1989 Leonel L Mitchell, an Episcopalian, argued that to baptize infants but not to communicate them was an unscriptural attempt to 'get the best of both worlds' and usually got the worst of both.[181]

---

[174] John S. Pridmore 'The Child and the Eucharist' in *Modern Believing* NS XXXIV (1992) pp.15-23, esp p.23.

[175] T.Gallant, *op.cit* p.154.

[176] *ibid* pp.191f.

[177] Cf also, not mentioned in the text, William R. Crockett, 'Theological Foundations for the Practice of Christian Initiation in the Anglican Communion' in David R. Holeton (ed), *Growing in Newness of Life* (Anglican Book Centre, Toronto, 1993) p.51, and Jeffrey J. Meyers, *The Lord's Service: The Grace of Covenant Renewal Worship* (Canon Press, Moscow, Id, 2003) p.393. From the 1990s the debate was particularly strong among conservative Presbyterians, and for a good summary of the arguments on both sides, cf Keith A. Mathison, *Given for You* (P & R Publishing, Phillipsburg, New Jersey, 2003) pp.313-24.

[178] J.B.Jordan, *Theses on Paedocommunion* p.1.

[179] H.Frederick Reisz jr, 'Infant Communion: A Matter of Christian Unity' in *Word and World*, Minnesota, VIII (1988) pp.63-65.

[180] R.S.Rayburn in 'Report of the Ad-Interim Committee to study the Question of Paedocommunion: Minority Report',1988, in *Position Papers*, pp.502-14.   .

[181] Leonel L.Mitchell, 'The Communion of Infants and Little Children' in *Anglican Theological Review* LXXI (1989) pp.63-78, reprinted in Ruth A. Meyers (ed) *op.cit* pp.165-87, esp p.174.

In 1991 Glenn Davies urged, 'Our covenant children are members of Christ's body and share in Christ. They should therefore share in the one bread and drink the same cup of blessing which we drink.'[182] In 1992 Peter Leithart wrote that 'baptism admits the baptized child to the Table of the covenant Lord'. Children did not enjoy such privileges of covenant membership as voting or holding office, but this 'in no way implies that they should be excluded from the covenant meal.'[183] In 1999 Maxwell E. Johnson, a Lutheran, wrote that the recovery of 'a foundational understanding of baptism as entry to the Eucharistic companionship of the church' calls for the communion of all the baptized[184], and he later added explicitly that this should apply 'even within the rites of initiation for infants.'[185]

Gallant argued from 1 Corinthians 12.13 that with baptism as an initiation into the *koinonia* and the Lord's table a particular manifestation of this, 'it is impossible to grant the one without the other.'[186] Indeed, 'it is doubtful whether we can speak of our children as fully initiated into the covenant until they have received the sacrament of communion.'[187] Most recently, in 2006 Gregg Strawbridge, another reformed Presbyterian, urged,

> Theological consistency, historical precedent, challenges with practical and conceptual exclusion, and covenant signs and promises – all of these require an inclusion of the children of the faithful at the font and the table. Covenant children are members of the church. Let the lament no longer arise – "The young children ask for bread, but no one breaks it for them".'[188]

But not all have been convinced. In 1969 Wainwright recognized the logic of full infant initiation, but observed that churches which practised it were closely-knit communities where church and society were broadly coterminous or where the environment was hostile or indifferent. Where children would probably live their whole lives formally as Christians, there was a case for total infant initiation. But the patterns with which these

---

[182] Glenn N.Davies, *art. cit.* p.19.

[183] P.Leithart, *Daddy, why was I Excommunicated?* (Transfiguration Press, Niceville, Florida, 1992) p.74. Leithart was replying to Leonard J. Coppes, cf note 220 *infra*. An abridged version of this reply was published under the same title in *Rite Reasons: Studies in Worship, no.20*, (Biblical Horizons, April 1992)

[184] Maxwell E. Johnson in *The Rites of Christian Initiation* (Pueblo, Collegeville, Minnesota), 1999, pp.374-76.

[185] Maxwell E.Johnson, *ibid*, second edn, 2007, pp.459-63.

[186] T.Gallant, *op.cit.* p.36.

[187] *ibid* p.139.

[188] Gregg Strawbridge, 'The Polemics of Infant Communion' in G.Strawbridge (ed), *The Case for Covenant Communion* (Athanasius Press, Monroe, Louisiana) pp.147-66. The reference is to Lam. 4.4.

churches had been associated were being swept away, and eventually they would have to ask whether it was right to continue infant initiation when it was increasingly uncertain whether their infants would remain in the church.[189]

A different position was advocated in 1971 by Roger T. Beckwith. Water as in baptism was suitable for infants but bread and wine - solid food and intoxicant - were not. In any case, baptism was not complete without the ministry of the word and the faith this evokes, hence teaching and profession of faith are also prerequisites of communion.[190] In 1977 George Carey argued similarly that in infant baptism 'sacramental initiation is *incomplete*' because personal confession of faith was missing.[191] In 1987 C. FitzSimons Allison urged the importance of 'nurture in the Word' and the response of faith, and claimed that 'to communicate infants when we already have a sacrament of infant incorporation, which is baptism, confuses and conflates the place of baptism and Holy Communion as treated in the New Testament.'[192] In 1988 Walter E. Pilgrim, a Lutheran, argued that 'with the Eucharist, the responsibility of life within the family is present, and this makes sense only where conscious faith is present.'[193] In 1988 A.A. Langdon agreed that baptism constituted eligibility 'provided the conditions of readiness' were met. But integral to these were repentance, faith and obedience, which are 'proleptically present' in baptism, but for communion are required 'both *personally* and *repeatedly*'. Communion is both 'a matter of *personal* faith' and of '*public* affirmation'.[194] In the same year, conservative Presbyterians reaffirmed the difference between passive baptism and active communion.[195] In 1995 A. Daunton-Fear saw infant baptism as only 'provisional' until the child could affirm personal faith at the age of

[189] G.Wainwright, *op.cit*. pp.21, 24ff, 56f, 82f.
[190] Roger T.Beckwith, 'The Age of Admission to Communion' in *The Churchman*, LXXXV (1971), pp. 13-31; 'The Age of Admission to the Lord's Supper' in *Westminster Theological Journal*, Philadelphia, XXXVIII (1976) pp.123-51. Cf more recently R.T. Beckwith and A. Daunton-Fear, *The Water and the Wine: A Contribution to the Debate on Children and Holy Communion* (Latimer Studies 61, Latimer Trust, London, 2005), pp.24-29 and 39.
[191] G.L.Carey, 'Christian Beginning' in J. Stott (ed), *Obeying Christ in a Changing World* (Fount, London, 1977) p.135.
[192] C.FitzSimons Allison, 'Anglican Initiatory Rites: A Contribution to the Current Debate' in *Anglican and Episcopal History* LVI (1987) pp.17-43, esp p.37.
[193] Walter E.Pilgrim, 'Infant Communion: A Matter of Christian Concern' in *Word and World*, VIII (1988) p. 64.
[194] A.A.Langdon, *Communion for Children? The Current Debate* (Latimer Studies 28, Latimer House, Oxford, 1988) esp p.6.
[195] 'Report of the Ad-Interim Committee to study the Question of Paedocommunion',1988, in *Position Papers*, PCA Historical Centre 2003, pp.498-502.

discretion[196], and in 1999 Donald Allister repeated that infant baptism was 'incomplete, partial or provisional initiation'. Full membership 'comes when we respond, verbally and publicly, to the grace of God' through confirmation or something similar, and the baptized infant should be seen only as a probationary member.[197]

2. Infants were admitted to the Passover and other meals in the old covenant, and the communal nature of the eucharist requires that they be admitted to this too.

Keidel put forward a strong case that the only requisite for eating the passover was 'physical capability'.[198] C.H.B.Byworth in 1972 accepted that it began as a family meal but later became a pilgrimage feast at which the presence of children was not obligatory; but it was still possible that children capable of eating an 'olive's bulk' of meat took part.[199] In the same year Robert Davidson of the Church of Scotland noted that here 'through a combination of words, visual signs and actions - sharing the meal - the child participates in, and is nurtured in, the faith of the family and the community to which he belongs.'[200] Jordan claimed that 'The entire assumption of the Old Testament is that the whole family participated in the Passover.'[201]

Keidel argued again that infants were privileged to eat the other sacrificial meals of the old covenant such as peace offerings and the Feasts of Weeks and of Tabernacles.[202] Leithart [203] and Rayburn[204] agreed, and Jordan also

[196] A. Daunton-Fear, 'Resisting the Tide: Christian Initiation and Communion Reconsidered' in *Theology* XCVIII (1995) pp.273-82.

[197] Donald Allister, 'Admitting Children to Holy Communion' in *Churchman* CXIII (1999) pp.298ff. Allister's position was quickly criticised by Alan Ward in 'Communion before Confirmation: A Response to "Admitting Children to Holy Communion"'in *Churchman,* CXIV (2000) pp. 295-99. Ward thought that baptism alone could suffice for children who had appropriate understanding but were not yet ready for confirmation.

[198] C.L.Keidel, *art.cit,* pp.307-22. I have examined the arguments of Byworth and Keidel along with Beckwith's replies (see p.39 *infra)* more fully in *Infant Communion: The New Testament to the Reformation,* pp.7-9.

[199] C.H.B.Byworth, *Communion, Confirmation and Commitment* (Grove Booklet on Ministry and Worship 8, Grove Books, Bramcote, 1972) pp.12-15.

[200] Robert Davidson, 'Children in the Community of Faith - the Old Testament Context' in David G. Hamilton and Finlay A.J. Macdonald (eds), *op.cit,* p.9.

[201] J.B.Jordan, *op.cit* para.6.

[202] C.L.Keidel, *art.cit* pp.335f.

[203] P.Leithart, *op.cit* p.24f; cf also his 'Sacramental Hermeneutics and the Ceremonies of Israel' in G. Strawbridge (ed) *op.cit.* pp.111-130.

[204] Robert S. Rayburn, 'Defense of Paedocommunion'; address delivered in 2004 and published in J.A Pipa jnr and C.N. Willborn (eds), *The Covenant: God's Voluntary Condescension* (Presbyterian Press, Taylors, SC, 2005) pp.149-52.

mentioned the wilderness manna [205] stressed the 'all' in 1 Corinthians 10: 'The children, like many of the adults, may not have had complete understanding of the meaning of the manna ... yet they *all* ate'.[206] Matthew W. Mason saw passover meal, peace offerings, wilderness manna and bread of the presence as all typologically related to the supper, hence the case that baptized covenant children should have access to the supper is 'overwhelming'.[207]

Jordan[208], Gallant[209] and Ray R. Sutton, a Reformed Episcopalian,[210] cited Matthew 19.13f as indicating the covenant status of children and their right to the supper, while Von-Allmen cited Matthew 14.21 where their presence at the feeding of the multitude is 'an explicit attestation that the bread of life is meant for children also.' Von-Allmen further argued that to expel children from the table because they are children was to make the church 'a school for intellectuals', and that segregations appropriate for catechesis 'distort the nature of the Church when applied to the liturgy'.[211] Robinson told how his own children eventually pleaded 'It would help if I could have the bread and wine too' and argued that there was nothing that a child could not *receive* sacramentally. He could not *give* a responsible commitment, but this related to ministry rather than membership.[212] Macdonald urged 'our understanding of the church as a community of which children are members' and 'the understanding of children themselves and of their place within the church'.[213] In 1982 David G. Hamilton urged that 'The faith community is incomplete without the presence and participation of the young'. Like the adult, the child has much to learn, much to teach and gifts to share: 'It is not that *he* is the child and *we* are the Church. He is the child in the Church of which we too are part.'[214]

There were gains for all here. In 1980 Sutcliffe quoted an adult testimony, 'That our children celebrate with us in holy communion has

[205] J. B. Jordan, *op.cit.* para.8; cf also 'Children and the Religious Meals of the Old Creation' in Gregg Strawbridge (ed), *op.cit.* p.68..
[206] Glenn N.Davies, *art. cit.* p.16.
[207] Matthew W.Mason, 'Covenant Children and Covenant Meals: Biblical Evidence for Infant Communion' in *Churchman* CXXI (2007) 1.127-38
[208] James B.Jordan, *op.cit.* para.8.
[209] Tim Gallant, *op.cit* pp.23-26; cf also his 'The Kingdom of God and Children at the Table' in Gregg Strawbridge (ed) *op.cit.* p.42.
[210] Ray R.Sutton, 'Christ's Way-Bread for a Child' in Gregg Strawbridge (ed), *op.cit* p.85.
[211] J.J.Von-Allmen, *op.cit*, pp.186f.
[212] J.A.T.Robinson, *art.cit*, pp.153 and 162.
[213] Finlay A.J.MacDonald, *art.cit*, pp.560-64.
[214] David G. Hamilton, 'The Place of the Child in the Church - historical perspectives' in David G. Hamilton and Finlay A.J. Macdonald (eds), *op.cit*, p. 27.

changed us'.[215]   In 1981 Holeton argued that 'Once all the community shares in the eucharist the experience becomes a conversion.'[216]   In 1983 White urged that 'The presence of children at the Lord's Table reminds adult Christians of how much growth lies ahead of us' and that this might be their 'special form of priestly ministry'.[217]   In 1993 two Canadian Anglicans, Gregory Kerr-Wilson and Timothy Perkins, claimed that the eucharist would be seen more clearly, the church would no longer be perceived as an exclusively adult community and, although there would be less silence, the quality of worship would be transformed.[218]

Again, not all were convinced.   Beckwith admitted that Exodus 12.14 implied that children, though not infants, partook at the first Passover but he emphasized that the requirement was later restricted to adult males; only at the beginning of the second century AD were women and children again required to participate.[219]   In 1988 Leonard J. Coppes also distinguished between the two Passovers and denied that children participated fully in the Old Testament sacrificial meals.[220]   Traditional Presbyterians noted that most advocates agreed that 'a certain level of maturity' was necessary for participation in the Passover and, citing Hebrews 5.12-14, suggested that in the New Testament 'the degree of required maturity could be heightened.'[221]   Langton thought the Passover irrelevant in that the concept 'of the *vicarious and atoning* death of Christ ... has a quality of meaning far removed from that of the Old Testament Passover concept.' [222]

3. Communion is a means of grace and nourishment, and, biblically and educationally, experience precedes understanding.

Crawford claimed that psychologists could attest the value of communion for infants, while pastoral theologians could show the benefit to family life 'if "initiation" were into the deeper meaning of the sacraments, rather like

---

[215]   J.M.Sutcliffe, *art.cit* p.33.
[216]   David R.Holeton, *Infant Communion - Then and Now,* pp.15 and 24.   Cf also his 'The Communion of Infants and Young Children' in G Muller-Fahrenholz (ed), *op.cit,* pp.59-69.
[217]   James F.White, *The Sacraments as God's Self-Giving,* p.67.
[218]   Gregory Kerr-Wilson and Timothy Perkins, 'Consequences of Infant Communion' in *Growing in Newness of Life,* pp.63-71.
[219]   Roger T.Beckwith 'The Age of Admission to the Lord's Supper' esp pp.130-51; cf also *The Water and the Wine,* esp pp.16-23.
[220]   Leonard J.Coppes, *Daddy, May I take Communion?* (Leonard J. Coppes, Thornton, Colorado, 1988), *passim.*
[221]   'Report of the Ad-Interim Committee to study the Question of Paedocommunion', 1988, in *Position Papers,* pp.498-502.
[222]   A.A.Langton, *art. cit.* pp.20f.

the child's initiation into the mysteries of family meals.'[223]   Byworth
argued that if we were to keep the best till later, we would not encourage
children in prayer or bible-reading either.   If the supper is a means of
grace, it cannot be denied to them.[224]   Cyrille Argenti described the
practical outworkings of all this in an Orthodox parish.[225]   Macdonald
criticized the view of communion as the goal of Christian nurture and saw
'participation in the full sacramental life of the Church as a precious
means of grace' which encouraged the child to commitment.[226]   Torrance
claimed that

> 'the child is called to receive in faith that grace into which he or she
> has been baptized.   A child can respond to the call and by faith
> feed upon Christ (John 6).   The faith may be as a grain of mustard
> seed, and understanding minimal, but where a child can hear and
> understand something of the meaning of the words, "Take, eat ...",
> who can forbid him?'[227]

Eastman wrote, 'As babies have no need to understand the dynamics of
parental love in order to sense, to know that they are loved through touch,
sight, and sound, so they do not need to have a theological grasp of the
eucharist in order to be fed by it'.[228]   Hamilton, drawing on James W.
Fowler, also argued for 'the wholeness of faith' against its restriction to
intellectual assent.   'The question of coming to the Table in faith has to
do not so much with having arrived as with taking nourishment for the
journey.   If faith is the gift of God then so also is the increase in faith.
And nowhere is the gift more graciously proffered than at the Table of our
Lord'.[229]   Later, Rayburn urged that 'something one must always see to on
behalf of newborns is their nourishment'[230], and Pridmore commented,
'Children 'say "Abba" more easily than we do.   So if faith be a
prerequisite of receiving the sacrament then many a child is more entitled
to do so than are adults.'[231]

---

[223]   Charles Crawford, *art. cit.* p.524 n.4.
[224]   C.H.B.Byworth, *op.cit.* pp.12-15.
[225]   Cyrille Argenti, 'Children and the Eucharist' in G.Muller-Fahrenholz (ed), *op.cit.* pp.57ff.
[226]   Finlay A.J.MacDonald, *art.cit* p.557.
[227]   T.Torrance, *art.cit* p.6.
[228]   A.T.Eastman, *op.cit* p.26.
[229]   David G.Hamilton, 'Faith Development, Christian Education and the Lord's Supper' in David G.
        Hamilton and Finlay A.J. Macdonald (eds), *op.cit*, pp.28-32, esp p.32.   Fowler's best-known work
        is *Stages of Faith: The Psychology of Human Development and the Quest for Meaning* (Harper
        and Row, San Francisco, 1981).
[230]   R.S.Rayburn, Minority Report, p.507;   cf also his 'Defense of Paedocommunion' in J.A Pipa jnr and
        C.N. Willborn (eds), *op.cit* pp.158f.
[231]   John Pridmore, *art.cit* p.22.

In 1987 Mark Searle urged that the model for Christian learning was 'closer to that of an apprenticeship than that of a classroom'. Here, the accent was on doing 'which makes the practice of withholding from small children the anointing of the Spirit and regular participation at the Eucharistic table all the more unfortunate.'[232]   In 1988 Ruth A Meyers, again drawing on Fowler, argued that the heart of faith was the experience of 'trust, a capacity which is present at birth and which begins to develop as soon as a child begins interacting with those around her, that is, also at birth.'   The church recognized this in baptizing infants and incorporating them into the faith community, and to admit them to the eucharist, the central act in its ongoing life, was to offer the means by which they could be nurtured in faith.'[233]   Mitchell observed of the 'ignorance' of children that

> 'Ignorance in the sense of unwillingness to learn is not at question here, but rather inexperience, innocence, and the inability to comprehend.   Yet compared to the truth of the mystery of redemption, the difference between what I understand and what the infant understands is as the difference in distance between leaving from New York and leaving from Tokyo on a trip to Mars.   While from my earthbound perspective it may appear large, it is but a tiny fraction of the total.'[234]

But, if children were to be helped here, Kerr-Wilson and Perkins claimed that infant communion offered a more natural way of learning. It

> 'shifts the direction of sacramental catechesis from information to formation.   A child's first encounter with the eucharist will not be instruction about what they are going to be allowed to do, but an experience of receiving the body and blood of Christ in the context of the eucharistic community.   Children will not so much learn *about* the eucharist as they will become inculturated *in* the worship life of the church.'[235]

Gallant urged that 'The Supper communicates truth that a child may not be able to articulate clearly, but that does not mean that he has no apprehension whatsoever'.   In the household, a two-year-old might not be

[232] Mark Searle, 'Introduction' and 'Infant Baptism Reconsidered' in Mark Searle (ed), *Alternative Futures for Worship, Volume 2: Baptism and Confirmation* (Liturgical Press, Collegeville, Minnesota,1987) pp.13 and 49.

[233] Ruth A Meyers, 'Infant Communion: Reflections on the Case from Tradition' in *Anglican and Episcopal History* LVII (1988) pp.159-75, reprinted in her (ed) *Children at the Table* p.146-64; cf esp pp.160f.

[234] L.L.Mitchell, *art. cit.* p.173

[235] Gregory Kerr-Wilson and Timothy Perkins, *art.cit.* p.64.

able to say much about how food gets to the table, but he knows almost instinctively that it comes from his parents and he grows in that knowledge. Similarly with the sacrament. The child 'can learn very early that in some way the Lord Jesus is feeding him, and grows in that knowledge.'[236] In 2005 Rich Lusk argued that to withhold the supper from children is 'to starve the very faith we are called to feed and nourish.'[237]

But again there were objections. Carey urged that if communion was the central service, 'The child can be taught that ... he must wait until he can make a public and self-conscious act of commitment'[238], and in 1980 John Tiller argued that,

> 'We do not simply share a meal with Jesus, but a meal on Jesus, a communion in his Body and Blood. The reception of the bread and wine as that Body and Blood, made so explicitly in the eucharistic texts, is unintelligible to a young child except in the most crudely literal sense. It is irrelevant to object that none of us, however adult, can fully understand this. It is still worse to point to the capacity a child has for wonder and imagination. That is just the trouble. The words are there in the service, and the child's imagination will get to work to try to make something of them. What emerges, however fantastic, will nevertheless be quite literal because children under twelve are only capable of what the psychologists call "concrete conceptions".'[239]

In 1987 Allison thought that the ideal of children never knowing a time when they did not communicate sounded like 'programming people'[240], and Langton claimed that 'the child is not disadvantaged by non-admission to the Holy Communion ... provided his incorporation into the loving relationships of a Christian family and of the local congregation is a genuine reality in everyday experience.'[241] Mark Tranvik, a Lutheran, argued that communion was 'a meal of forgiveness for those who have willfully broken their relationship with Christ', and infants simply did not need this.[242]

---

[236] T.Gallant, op.cit p.162. Cf also 'The Kingdom of God and Children at the Table' in G. Strawbridge (ed), op.cit., pp.35-48.

[237] Rich Lusk, Paedofaith (Athanasius Press, Monroe, Louisiana, 2005) pp.115f.

[238] G.L.Carey 'Christian Beginning' in J. Stott (ed), op.cit. p.138.

[239] J.Tiller 'Justification and the Sacraments' in A.P. Baker, G.L.Carey, J. Tiller and N.T.Wright, The Great Acquittal (Fount, London, 1980) pp.57f.

[240] C.FitzSimons Allison, art.cit. p.36.

[241] A.A.Langton, art.cit. esp. p. 39.

[242] Mark Tranvik, 'Should Infants be Communed? A Lutheran Perspective' in Word & World XV (1995) p. 89.

4. 1 Corinthians 11 is irrelevant to children

Keidel argued that 'there is nothing said in 1 Corinthians 11 which *necessitates* the application of Paul's requirements to infants and children'. Words such as 'whoever' and 'anyone' are used in a limited sense elsewhere in scripture, and it should not be assumed that this is not the case here.[243] Later, Rayburn observed that 'we do not understand Acts 2.39 to deny baptism to little children, Romans 10.13-14 to deny them salvation, or 2 Thessalonians 3.10 to deny them food.'[244]

Brand urged that 1 Corinthians 11, if applied to children, 'must mean their ability to understand themselves as interrelated with a community - a relationship like their family.   That perception comes - at least in its most basic form - early in childhood.'[245] Weatherhead saw the context as the unity of the body.   A child accepted into the worship of the church would *feel* that he is part of the worshipping community and 'in a real sense discern the body', while if we exclude children, 'are we not failing to discern the Body in that we fail to discern that the Body includes the children?'[246] Norman M. Pritchard, also from the Church of Scotland, argued that 1 Corinthians 11 was concerned with adult 'self-appraisal'.[247] Karl-Heinrich Bieritz saw it as requiring '*conduct* appropriate to the reality of the "body of Christ" in the twofold sense of this term.'   Since baptized children belong to this body 'without qualification and with full entitlement', it may be that by excluding them we are 'equally guilty of failing to "discern the body" and therefore of endangering the reality of the supper as were the Corinthians by their unbrotherly conduct.'[248] Jordan argued that its concern was not intellectual but moral.   Its context was the sin of schism – and one of fullest expressions of that sin is to exclude children[249], while Young claimed that children *can* 'discern the body', and to divide it on the ground of age was to destroy its unity, 'Perhaps it is we who fail to "discern the body" when we do not welcome our children to communion'.   And in 'children' he specifically included infants.[250] Buchanan stressed that discernment was not primarily

[243] C.L.Keidel, *art.cit.* pp.332-36.
[244] R.S.Rayburn in Minority Report, p.509.
[245] Eugene L.Brand, *art. cit*, pp.29-42.
[246] James L.Weatherhead, *art.cit*, p.8.
[247] Norman M.Pritchard, 'Profession of Faith and Admission to Communion in the light of 1 Corinthians 11 and other passages' in *Scottish Journal of Theology* XXXIII (1980) pp.55-70.
[248] Karl-Heinrich Bieritz, 'The Lord's Supper as Sacrament of Fellowship' in G Muller-Fahrenholz (ed), *op.cit.* pp.38-50, esp p.45.
[249] James B.Jordan, *Theses on Paedocommunion*, paras.14 and 19.
[250] Daniel Young, *op.cit.* cf esp. pp.4-6, 12 and 16.

cognitive; the Corinthian failure was a moral one, and self-examination must be related to the capacity to sin.[251]   Rayburn urged that Paul was warning against 'impious and irreverent participation', and much more would be needed 'before it could be concluded that Paul was speaking to the general question of who may come to the table.[252]   Jeffrey Meyers saw the context as the unity of the body, and, if children were excluded, 'we eat as a divided body' and 'a great big ugly division is manifest at the table'.   Those guilty of not 'discerning the Lord's body' were not children who lacked intellectual maturity but those who barred them.[253] Leithart claimed that the proclamation was the communal action of eating and drinking, and that the remembrance lay primarily in the doing.[254]

Again, not all were convinced.   Coppes claimed that proclamation of the Lord's death was a 'personal and not simply a communal declaration' and that 'remembrance' denoted a self-conscious act.[255]   Pilgrim argued that the passage assumed 'a community of people able to think and reflect on what they are doing in relation to the body of Christ (the church and the Eucharist).'[256] Daunton-Fear argued that 'discerning the body' referred to the communion bread[257], and Transvik suspected that it meant discerning 'the presence of Christ in the bread'.[258]   In 2005 Kenneth Gentry jnr admitted that Paul's concern was to oppose 'impious and irreverent' adult participation.   But 'the act of remembering Jesus' person and word' is beyond the capacity of a child: 'An infant may be held in the arms of the pastor and baptized, but he cannot respond to the command to "take", "eat", "drink" – all while responsibly remembering and applying the Lord's death and his coming judgment to his own condition.'   Hence 'the Lord's Supper must be withheld from the covenant child until he can partake responsibly and with understanding.'[259]

[251] C.O.Buchanan, *Children in Communion*, pp.11ff.
[252] R.S.Rayburn, Minority Report, p. 509,   cf also his 'Defense of Paedocommunion' in J.A Pipa jnr and C.N. Willborn (eds), *op.cit.* pp.153-56.
[253] Jeffrey J. Meyers, *Presbyterian, Examine Thyself* , Rite Reasons: Studies in Worship 47, Septermber 1996.   cf also his 'Presbyterian, Examine Thyself: Restoring Children to the Table' in G. Strawbridge (ed), *op.cit*, pp.19-34, esp p.20. Cf also T. Gallant, *op.cit.* pp.72-105.
[254] P.Leithart, *op.cit.* esp. pp.24f.
[255] L.J.Coppes, *op. cit.* pp.18f.
[256] W.E.Pilgrim, *art.cit* p.62.
[257] A. Daunton-Fear, *art.cit* pp.276f.
[258] M.Transvik, *art.cit* p.86.
[259] Kenneth Gentry jr, 'Pauline Communion vs Paedocommunion' in Joseph A Pipa jr and C.N. Willborn (eds), *op.cit.* pp.163-210.

5. The Last Fifty Years: (ii) Church Responses

Ecumenical Dimensions

Participants in a World Council of Churches 1980 consultation at Bag Segeberg were 'rather strongly in favour of earlier admission'[260], and their report saw 'no theological reason for excluding any baptized persons from communion, whatever their age.'[261]   In 1990 another WCC report noted that many churches saw the relation of baptism and eucharist as 'so intrinsic, that baptized children should be admitted to eucharistic communion', though due instruction was 'a pedagogical and catechetical necessity.'[262]

The Roman C.atholic Church

In 1971 Rome apparently ruled out infant communion by still requiring confession before first communion.   It permitted certain variations 'for the time being'[263], but in 1973 it disallowed these[264] and in 1977 maintained firmly that confession must precede first communion.[265]   In the 1983 Code of Canon Law, canon 912 provided that 'Any baptized person who is not prohibited by law can and must be admitted to Holy Communion', but canon 913 immediately qualified this by requiring that children have sufficient knowledge 'to understand the mystery of Christ according to their capacity.'   Most commentators give priority to the right of the baptized, hence 'a doubt about the use of reason or sufficient disposition should be resolved in favour of the child's receiving communion.'[266]   The 1994 *Catechism of the Catholic Church* repeated that 'Children must go to the sacrament of Penance before receiving Holy Communion for the first time'[267], but this is clearly a matter of discipline

---

[260] WCC, ... *and do not hinder them*, p.1.

[261] *ibid*. pp.4-19.

[262] *Baptism, Eucharist & Ministry 1982-1990: Report on the Process and Responses*, Faith and Order Paper no. 149 (Geneva, 1990) pp.109ff.

[263] Congregation for the Clergy, Addendum to *General Catechetical Directory*, 11 Apr 1971, no.5, *Acta Apostolicae Sedis* LXIV (1972) pp.97-176.

[264] Sacred Congregation for the Discipline of the Sacraments, *Declaration on children's confession prior to their first communion*, 24 May 1973, *AAS* LXV (1973) pp.410.

[265] Sacred Congregation for the Sacraments and Divine Worship and Sacred Congregation for the Clergy, *Letter* to *the conferences of bishops, on children's first confession prior to first communion*, 31 Mar 1977, ET *The Tablet*, 28 May 1977, pp.514f.

[266] J.A.Coriden, T.J. Green and D.E. Heintschel (eds), *The Code of Canon Law: A Text and Commentary* (Geoffrey Chapman, London, 1985) pp.651-53.

[267] Para. 1457 (ET, Geoffrey Chapman, London, 1994) p.327.

rather than doctrine, for the 1990 *Codex Canonum Ecclesiarum Orientalium* for eastern churches in communion with Rome reaffirmed that after baptism and chrismation the eucharist is to be administered 'as soon as possible', though 'suitable precautions' were to be taken with infants.[268] In 1996 the Congregation for Eastern Churches explained further that infants were not to be communicated only at initiation:

> 'Eucharist is the Bread of Life, and infants need to be nourished constantly, from then on, to grow spiritually. The method of their participation in the Eucharist corresponds to their capacity: they will initially be different from the adults, inevitably less aware and not very rational, but they will progressively develop, through the grace and pedagogy of the sacrament.'[269]

Subsequently R.J.B. Flummerfelt has argued that in certain circumstances a Latin presbyter would be right to communicate at initiation and subsequently the infant child of members of an Uniate church if they have no access to a parish of that church.[270]

The Church of England

In 1971 the Ely report urged admission prior to confirmation but after 'adequate preparation'[271], and in the wake of it General Synod agreed in 1974 that communion 'may precede a mature Profession of Faith', though again instruction was required first.[272] In 1985 the Knaresborough report *Communion before Confirmation?* stated that 'to be capable of receiving baptism is to be capable of receiving communion' and noted the anomaly in the Alternative Service Book where an infant baptized at the eucharist was formally welcomed into the body of Christ but denied participation in it a few minutes later. Its logic here implied infant communion – but from 1 Corinthians 11 it required 'some awareness of both the corporate nature of the Church and the significance of the Eucharist itself', though it accepted that this awareness is 'according to the capacity of the person

---

[268] Canons 697 and 710, ET *Code of Canons of the Eastern Churches: Latin-English Edition* (Canon Law Society of America, Washington DC, 2001) pp. 266f, 272.

[269] *Instruction for Applying the Liturgical Prescriptions of the Code of Canons of the Eastern Churches* (Vatican, 1996) n.51, reproduced in *Eastern Christian Publications* (Fairfax, Virginia, 1996).

[270] R.J.B.Blummerfelt, *Baptism, Chrismation, and Eucharist for infants: Questions of Rights and Rites, A Thesis submitted to the Faculty of the School of Religious Studies of The Catholic University of Washington* 1999.

[271] *Christian Initiation: Birth and Growth in the Christian Society* (GS 30, CIO, 1971), paras. 119-21, p.42 and para 157, p.48.

[272] *Report of Proceedings* V (1974) 1.272-292. *Christian Initiation: Birth and Growth in the Christian Society*

involved' and it noted that many Orthodox understood this simply as 'an awareness of being loved'.[273]

In 1995 *On the Way* included some answers to objections to the earlier admission of children[274], and in 1996 the bishops issued a report reaffirming the traditional pattern as the norm but allowing communion before confirmation in accordance with some draft guidelines.[275]   General Synod welcomed this[276], and in 1997 the bishops confirmed the guidelines with only minor amendments.   These stated that 'the time of the first receiving should be determined not so much by the child's chronological age, as by his or her appreciation of the significance of the sacrament', but they did require 'an appropriate and serious pattern of preparation'.[277]   In 2000 Synod asked for a report within five years on the implementation of the guidelines[278], and in 2005 the Education Division reported that 1650 churches in 36 dioceses were admitting unconfirmed children and that many dioceses had settled for an age around seven, though Oxford had designated a minimum age of four.   It concluded with some recommended new draft regulations.[279]   The report and regulations were initially approved by General Synod in 2005[280], and the bishops then issued slightly revised regulations[281] and these were finally approved in Synod that year.[282]

The new regulations allow the admission of baptized children who are neither ready nor desirous to be confirmed where parishes request this and where diocesan bishops are willing to consider such requests. Before granting such permissions, the bishop is to satisfy himself
> '(a) that the parish concerned has made adequate provision for preparation and continuing nurture in the Christian life and will encourage any child admitted to Holy Communion under these Regulations to be confirmed at the appropriate time and (b) where the parish concerned is within the area of a local ecumenical project ... that the other participating Churches have been consulted.'

---

[273] *Communion before Confirmation?* (CIO, 1985) para 2.6, pp.7f, and para 7.3, pp.36f.
[274] *On the Way* (GS Misc 444, CHP, 1995) paras 5.47 -5.57, pp.92-97.
[275] *Admission to Communion in Relation to Baptism and Confirmation: Report by the House of Bishops,* GS 1212
[276] *Report of Proceedings* XXVII (1996) pp.964-1001.
[277] *Admission of Baptized Persons to Holy Communion before Confirmation: Revised Guidelines agreed by the House of Bishops,* GS Misc 488.
[278] *Report of Proceedings* XXXI (2000) 3.236.
[279] *Children and Holy Communion: A Review* (GS 1576)
[280] *Report of Proceedings* XXXVI (2005) 2.174-95; 3.87-99
[281] *Admission of Baptized Children to Holy Communion Regulations 2006* (GS 1596A)
[282] *Report of Proceedings* XXXVII (2006) 1.155-72.

Equally, the incumbent must be satisfied that the child has been baptized and that someone with parental responsibility is content that he/she should be admitted. Otherwise, 'subject to any direction of the bishop', the incumbent has absolute discretion to decide whether and when a child should first be admitted. Significantly there is no reference to a minimum age and, although the debate centred on young children, there was an approving reference by the Bishop of Durham to 'babes in arms'. Subsequently the Bishop of Dover who piloted the resolutions through Synod declared, 'If I were pushed I would opt to give children communion from baptism much as the Orthodox Church does.'[283]

The Wider Anglican Communion

In 1970 American liturgists urged that, 'Those who have been made members of the family of God have the right to be fed at the Lord's table ... Those who are admitted by Baptism into the Communion of Saints should be allowed to partake of the Holy Communion.'[284] A small child often had a natural recognition of the sacrament but even without this 'Communion becomes an integral part of the child's Christian experience from the beginning. He can never remember when he was not fed at the table of the Lord.'[285] But, as Louis Weil complained, the 1979 *Book of Occasional Services* did not state whether there should be a specific age for first communion, nor did it indicate explicitly whether the first reception should be at the child's baptism.[286] By now other provinces including Wales, New Zealand and Australia were concerned[287], and in 1985 the first International Anglican Liturgical Consultation, held in Boston, Mass., deemed it paradoxical

> 'to admit children to membership in the body of Christ through baptism, and yet to deny that membership in the eucharistic meal that follows.

---

[283] Interview in Stephen Lake, *Let the Children come to Communion* (SPCK, London, 2006) p.93.

[284] *Holy Baptism with the Laying-on-of-Hands, Prayer Book Studies 18: On Baptism and Confirmation* (Church Pension Fund, New York, 1970) p.18. Cf also Daniel B. Stevick, 'Christian Initiation: Post-Reformation to the Present Era' in *Made, Not Born*, pp.115f.

[285] *ibid*, p. 21.

[286] Louis Weil, 'Disputed Aspects of Infant Communion'in *Studia Liturgica* XVII (1987) pp.256-63.

[287] Cf D. R Holeton, 'Christian Initiation in some Anglican Provinces', *Studia Liturgica XII* (1977) pp.129-50; *Christian Initiation: A Report of the Doctrinal Commission of the Church in Wales* (Church in Wales Publications, np, 1971) *passim*; B. Davis, 'New Zealand Initiation Experience', in C.O. Buchanan (ed), *Nurturing Children in Communion* pp.23-29; B. Davis and T. Brown, 'New Zealand Initiation Experience' in Ruth.A. Meyers (ed), *op.cit* pp.85-98; R. L. Dowling, 'Pushing at the Door: (ii) The Anglican Church in Australia', *ibid* pp.107-11; 'Appendix 1: Communion of the Baptized but Unconfirmed in Anglicanism', *ibid* pp.194-98. We should now add Canada, Scotland and others to this list.

'to assert that communion is a "means of grace" and yet to insist that children must shows "signs of grace" before they be given the eucharistic "means of grace".

'to place further hurdles, whether of age, attainment, or sacramental rite of passage, before the candidate could begin communicant life.'

Some might desire a 'minimum age' as a half-way stage, but this might become a fixed solution and it did not take baptism 'sufficiently seriously as incorporation into the eucharistic life'. The report formally recommended that 'all baptized persons be admitted to communion'.[288]

The Anglican Consultative Council in 1987 asked whether 'the disciplinary requirements for receiving the sacrament' and the danger of unworthy receiving might preclude infants and young children.[289] But Americans were less hesitant, and a 1988 revision of *The Book of Occasional Services* specifically allowed – for the first time - the communion of a newly-baptized infant 'in the form of a few drops of wine'. Later that year General Convention agreed 'That those baptized in infancy, may, as full members of The Body of Christ, begin receiving communion at any time they desire and their parents permit.'[290] In 1991 the fourth International Anglican Liturgical Consultation, held in Toronto, reaffirmed the Boston statement and concluded that a minimum age 'should be only an interim step in transition to the norm of communion of all the baptized.'[291]

Some Protestant Churches
American Lutherans, in their 1978 *Lutheran Book of Worship*, saw communion as 'the birthright of the baptized' and suggested that children communicate with their families as soon as they 'begin to participate in the congregation's life'.[292] In 1997 they went further and affirmed that 'infants and children may be communed for the first time during the

---

[288] Cf *Nurturing Children in Communion*, pp.42-49. Most conference papers were published here, and several were republished (sometimes with revisions) in *Children at the Table* which also included further essays.

[289] *Many Gifts One Spirit. Report of ACC-7: Singapore 1987*, (Church House Publishing for ACC, London, 1987) pp.68-72.

[290] Quoted in L.L. Mitchell, *Worship: Initiation and the Churches* (Pastoral Press, Washington 1991) p.145.

[291] The Toronto report, 'Walk in Newness of Light' was first printed in D. R. Holeton (ed), *Christian Initiation in the Anglican Communion* (Grove Worship Series 118, Grove Books, Bramcote, 1991). It was reprinted, along with many of the conference papers, in D.R. Holeton (ed), *Growing in Newness of Life* (Anglican Book Centre, Toronto, 1993) pp.227-54, cf esp p.229 and 232.

[292] Quoted from L.L .Mitchell, *op.cit.* p.161.

service in which they are baptized' although regular communion thereafter could be deferred.[293]

In the reformed tradition, the 1970s saw discussion in the Church of Scotland[294] and a 1979 report urged the admission of 'baptized children capable of responding in faith'.[295]   The report and a discussion document, *Children – the Challenge to the Church,* were sent to the presbyteries for study, and another report in 1982 urged the admission of children on the grounds of the priority of grace, the sacrament as a fellowship meal, the nature of nurture and the strengthening of the family.[296]   This was approved by the General Assembly, but failed to receive adequate support from the presbyteries.   A further report, issued in 1991, upheld the 1982 arguments, gave careful attention to scripture and saw 'no substantive theological obstacle to the participation of baptized children' after 'a brief and simple form of preparation'.   There was no theological ground for a minimum age, although first communion would be unlikely 'before the early years in primary school' since the child should be able to cope physically with the handling of the elements, should not unduly disturb the good order of worship and above all should 'positively wish to take Communion in an awareness of the invitation of Jesus.'[297]   The report was accepted both by the General Assembly and by the presbyteries, and a Standing Act of 1992 formally authorized admission where a Kirk session was satisfied that baptized children 'are being nurtured within the life and worship of the Church and love the Lord and respond in faith to the invitation, "take, eat"'.   In England, the United Reformed church published two booklets c.1980 inviting congregations to consider whether children could receive communion.[298]   Later a report from the Children's Work Committee recommended 'that all children who are regularly part of the fellowship of the church be encouraged to take full part in communion, after preparation.'[299]

---

[293]   Cf M. E. Johnson, second edition, *op.cit.* pp.413f.

[294]   I am grateful here for help from the Rev Douglas Galbraith who also pointed me to the excellent summary in Finlay A. J. Macdonald, *Confidence in a Changing Church* (St Andrew Press, Edinburgh, 2004) pp.83-91.

[295]   *Reports* to the General Assembly of the Church of Scotland (1979) pp.410ff.

[296]   *The Lord's Supper and the Children of the Church* (Assembly Reports, 1982) pp.467-77.

[297]   *The Participation of Baptized Children in the Sacrament of the Lord's Supper* (Assembly Reports, 1991) pp.521-36.

[298]   *Together for Communion* and John M. Sutcliffe, *Communion - what children say* (Church Life Department, United Reformed Church, London, nd).

[299]   *Children in Communion?* (United Reformed Church, London, nd, c.1999) pp.9, 27

In 1973 the Methodist Conference considered a report which contemplated earlier admission, and in 1975 its Faith and Order Committee recognized that 'There is nothing in the constitution of Methodism which denies communion to children.'[300] In 1985 Conference affirmed that all the baptized 'are entitled to their place at the Lord's Table, though it may be expedient for this to be delayed.'[301] In 1987 Conference received another report, *Children at Holy Communion*, with guidelines which still insisted 'that there should be sufficient explanation and preparation, in relation to age and experience.'[302] It invited local churches to encourage fuller participation of children[303], and to assist them the Department of Education and Youth published in 1989 *Children at Holy Communion: One Body With Him* by Peter Sulston and Leigh Pope who were clear that 'The Lord's Supper is open to all who have been baptized.'[304] In 1997 another working party surveyed present practice which revealed that in a few churches children under five were being admitted[305], and in 2000 Conference adopted a report recommending that it become the normal practice for baptized children to communicate 'irrespective of age', though the consent of parents should be sought first.[306]

The Church of Scotland[307], Methodist[308] and United Reformed[309] reports, the Council of Churches for Britain and Ireland[310] and some individual writers[311] have considered the possibility of unbaptized children seeking communion. There are important issues here both pastoral and theological, but they are not likely to arise with infants.

[300] *Children and the Sacrament of Holy Communion: A compilation of the Conference statements on this subject in 1973, 1975 and 1978*, 1979.
[301] *Children at Holy Communion: Guidelines*, 1987, p.6.
[302] *ibid* pp.9f.
[303] *ibid* p.3.
[304] Peter Sulston and Leigh Pope, *Children at Holy Communion: One Body with Him*, p.47. This guide was based on Leigh Pope's earlier book, *Helping children participate in Holy Communion*
[305] Methodist Council, Children in Communion Working Party, pp.165-76.
[306] Resolution 15, *Minutes of Conference* 2000 (Methodist Conference Office, London) p.6.
[307] *Reports* to the General Assembly of the Church of Scotland (1979) p.412, cited F. Macdonald, *art.cit* p.599;
[308] *Children at Holy Communion: Guidelines*, 1987, p.9f.; *Methodist Council:* Children in Communion Working Party, p.171.
[309] *Children in Communion?*, pp.9, 27.
[310] *Baptism and Church Membership* (Churches Together in England, 1997) recommendations 89 and 90, pp.87f.
[310] J.M.Torrance, art. cit. p.7; C.O.Buchanan, *News of Liturgy*, no 228 (April 1997) pp.1-4.

6. Conclusions

No one in the west argues now that infant communion is absolutely necessary. But is it desirable? The practice was first attested only fifty years after the first clear attestation of infant baptism. The fathers never suggested requirements for communion which did not apply equally to baptism, and the two *may* have originated together even in New Testament times.[312] But it is a matter not simply of what existed in New Testament times – assuming, as is unlikely, a uniformity of practice then – but also of broader biblical principles. And, while Jeremy Taylor argued that 'The present practice of the church is to be our rule and measure of peace, and determination of the article'[313], today the practice of the church is divided.

Over the centuries the principal advocates of infant communion have held very different theologies, but there is a strong consensus in the substance of their arguments. Quite apart from the Lord's welcome of the children, baptized children are born again, they are members of the body of Christ and partakers of his body and blood, they are in a state of salvation, they are members of the church, the covenant community, and the eucharist cannot signify the unity of the body if they are excluded. It is clear that the ending of infant communion in the west was linked with an exaggerated concept of reverence, and that its earliest justifications – the need for the discretion of faith, the use of reason, actual devotion and reverence - were rationalizations rather than reasons. It is hard to resist the conclusion that they are still rationalizations, kept alive only by the unbiblical western idea of the church as a primarily adult body of which infants and children are only half-members.

To say that baptism is the sacrament of birth while the eucharist is the sacrament of growth, or that the eucharist is of use only to replace grace that has been lost, suggests that infants are spiritually static and implies a mechanistic view of grace; infants may not lose grace until they are guilty of actual sin, but they undergo new experiences every day and they cannot receive too much strengthening love, either human or divine.

---

[312] cf. Mark Dalby, *Infant Communion: The New Testament to the Reformation* pp.4-12
[313] See the arguments he deployed on p.11 above.

Of course they cannot actively take, eat, or drink 'in remembrance', but nor can they actively present themselves for baptism. If they cannot participate with subjective remembrance they can still share in an objective memorial action, and if they cannot consciously proclaim the Lord's death they may still do so in a real sense by the very act of participating. Again, infants cannot examine themselves or discern the Lord's body, but it is accepted by all that Paul's demands were directed to adults who had abused the sacrament, and the argument that they must also apply to infants is increasingly unconvincing. As Pridmore urged, the more we ponder the objections, 'the more insistent are the echoes of the original protest of the first disciples for whom the child's place was the circumference rather than the centre.'[314]

St Thomas accepted that baptized infants had a right to receive the body of Christ, but not immediately, 'just as they also have the right to receive an inheritance, although they do not take possession of it immediately.'[315] His argument is that not everything to which we have a right can be enjoyed at once, and that communion is most – or only? - beneficial after instruction and with understanding and faith. Beckwith and others argue that a formal profession of faith at confirmation is necessary before children can exercise their right, and the idea that this is a necessary part of initiation has had significant support in the past.[316] But it is possible to place too much emphasis on the 'formal'. An infant communicating trustfully is, in one sense, communicating in faith, and a very young child communicating with even a 'mustard seed' of understanding is making at least a partial profession of faith. Educationalists rightly stress that their experience *of* communion is more formative than instruction *about* it, and they are supported by the theological emphasis on communion as a means of nurture and grace. It is wiser therefore to see the profession of faith not primarily as a single act at an arbitrarily determined age, before which communion is inappropriate, but as something which begins in infancy and which hopefully continues and deepens throughout life.

Some writers have pressed for infant confirmation or chrismation as well as infant communion. I personally agree with them, but that is another matter. There still remains, however, the question of the age of infant admission. Those who argue for baptismal communion have logic on their side. Keidel and others who distinguished between infants and

---

[314] John Pridmore, *art. cit. p.21.*
[315] Aquinas, *Scriptum super Sententiis* IV dist ix a.5 q.4, ed M.F.Moos (Paris, 1947) iv.394-97.
[316] Cf, eg, A.M. Ramsey, 'The Doctrine of Confirmation' in *Theology* XLVIII (1945) p.201.

weaned children and argue for the communion only of those physically capable of eating may well be supported by the evidence of the Passover and other old covenant meals.   But this does not necessarily imply that baptismal communion is wrong and, if the communal nature of the eucharist requires admission as early as possible, we could well follow those who advocate immediate baptismal communion with future communions delayed until the child can eat and drink more naturally.   It is doubtful, though, except perhaps among Roman Catholics, whether a formal minimum age can be sustained.   Already advocacy of a lower but still post-instruction age is proving only an interim position, and infant communion as such is now becoming increasingly common.

Alcuin/GROW Joint Liturgical Studies

48-56 pages, £5.95 in 2008. Nos 1-58 by Grove Books Ltd, Ridley Hall Road, Cambridge CB3 9HU

Nos. 4,9 and 16 are out of print. Nos 59 and following are published by Hymns Ancient and Modern (previously named SCM-CanterburyPress Ltd) – see outside back cover

The Alcuin Club

promoting liturgical scholarship and renewal. More details on outside back cover and
at www.alcuinclub.org.uk. Recent publications include:

The Companion to Common Worship (two volumes)
edited by Paul Bradshaw
(Volume 1, SPCK 2001 - £19.99: Volume 2, SPCK 2006 - £19.99)

Celebrating Christ's Victory
by Benjamin Gordon-Taylor & Simon Jones
a practical guide to the celebration of the Christian Year
(SPCK 2005 - £9.99)

An Evangelical among the Anglican Liturgists
by Colin Buchanan
*a collection of the writings of one of the most influential evangelical liturgists of
our time*
(SPCK 2009 - £19.99)

Grove Liturgical Studies

*These Studies of 32-40 pages ran in 1975-86, commissioned by the Group for Renewal of Worship (see ouside
back cover) and published or distributed by Grove Books Ltd. Price in 2009, £3.50*

Grove Books Ltd, Ridley Hall Road, Cambridge CB3 9HU
Tel: 012223-464748 www.grovebooks.co.uk